CAMPAIGN IN EUROPE

THE STORY

OF

The 10th BATTALION
The HIGHLAND LIGHT INFANTRY
(CITY OF GLASGOW REGIMENT)

1944 - 1945

The Naval & Military Press Ltd

RECORDED BY

The Late Captain R. T. JOHNSTON
Captain D. N. STEWARD
and the Rev. A. IAN DUNLOP, *Chaplain*

Published by

The Naval & Military Press Ltd

Unit 5 Riverside, Brambleside
Bellbrook Industrial Estate
Uckfield, East Sussex
TN22 1QQ England

Tel: +44 (0)1825 749494

www.naval-military-press.com
www.nmarchive.com

Cover image:
Churchill tanks of 6th Guards Tank Brigade and troops of the 10th Highland Light Infantry,
15th (Scottish) Division, during the assault on Tilburg, Holland, 28 October 1944.

DEDICATED

To the memory of the fifteen officers
and two hundred and twenty six
other ranks of the Battalion who were
killed in action and died of wounds
during the campaign.

The history of a Unit can be recorded in two ways—in the dry, emotionless tone of the War Diary, or in the warmer, more human framework of a scrapbook. In the succeeding pages, it is intended to recall to mind incidents both before and during battle, not as the historian on a higher plane would regard them—small, rather meaningless actions amidst a welter of numerous other and similar ones—but as actions and happenings that characterise and give life-blood to what we know as The 10th Battalion The Highland Light Infantry. Names and dates must of necessity be an integral part but if an excuse be necessary, we justify our action by saying that it will constitute the only complete and compact record of our comrades who gave their lives or shed their blood for cause and country.

THE DISTANT DAYS

An off-shoot of the 5th Battalion, this unit found its early pre-war days ones of no small military bewilderment, while a shortage of equipment and men did not help in the striving towards fighting efficiency. But from earliest days, through the cold, cheerless winter of 1939-1940, and on into the militarily cheerless summer of 1940, through the dark days of the Shetlands and the isolation of Wick, the form it was ultimately to take and the glory it was ultimately to achieve took shape, gradually but surely, under the guiding hands of Lieut.-Colonels L. S. Morrison, T.D., F.A. Hawkins, M.C., T. W. Hamilton and R. G. Collingwood. It would take too long, nor would there be much point, to dwell on the early days when order came out of chaos—Danbury, Bradwell, Latchingdon, Cold Norton, Ipswich, Orford, The Shetlands, Watten. For the old-timers, these names will conjure up some memory, but they are of the past and have little relation to the Unit that fought in Normandy and beyond.

PRELUDE

Our story really begins when the Battalion left the wilds of Caithness for the slag heaps of Bedlington. For here it was that once again we became part of 15th (Scottish) Infantry Division, and with 2nd Battalion The Gordon Highlanders and 2nd Battalion The Argyll and Sutherland Highlanders formed 227 (Highland) Infantry Brigade. The tempo of training was speeded, new ideas were instilled, new methods took on and the whole atmosphere changed. This was Prelude to War.

August, 1943, saw the beginning of a friendship that was to bear great fruit a year later. It was at GANDALE, near Catterick, that we first met the 6th Guards Tank Brigade, whose place we had taken in the Division, and for ten days we worked and trained, talked and made friends with them. From these ten days, and another four spent with them in March, 1944, emerged the team that took us out of CAUMONT, to HERVIEUX, and the Second Army into the heart of the enemy defences.

September of that year (1943), saw us fully at home in the Division with our first full-scale exercise " Punchbowl," and the Games at lovely Rothbury. To say that " Punchbowl " was a great success would be to stretch the truth, but it taught us much and we benefited from its lessons.

And so to SLEDMERE (and FIMBER), the WOLDS, and Exercise " Blackcock," our first exercise with 8 Corps, Britain's new striking force. And here we gave a good account of ourselves, even if the Army Commander of that time was a little startled at our gallant, but naked, Company of river crossers. It is not on record but we imagine that the village they assailed was even more startled ! !

The rigours of " Blackcock " over, the Battalion shook off the mud of the wolds and took itself to the more urban delights of OTLEY. Here it was that Lieut.-Colonel R. G. Collingwood, for over a year the careful guide and teacher of the Battalion, left us and Major J. D. S. Young, D.S.O., M.C., assumed command. Major E. R. Colwill also joined us and the team that was to go to France was almost completed with the arrival of Major J. C. M. Stoker from the 13th Battalion. Our stay at OTLEY was characterised by periods of hard training—Exercises " Clansman " and " Eagle "—and moments of a more pleasing and lighter nature.

And so the months went by and the DAY came nearer ; all the time our progress was maintained and the Battalion took its final, fighting shape.

By mid-April, 1944, the music rose, the tone was louder, more strident, the orchestra was warming up for the prelude's final chord and the noisy opening of the work of WAR. Loading, unloading, Companies going overnight on strange schemes, security, secrecy, and then the move to the unknown destination and the final arrival in Sussex at Wiston Park, Steyning. More training, water-proofing, careful preparation, new kit, new weapons, new men ; the last final check before the great adventure, sunny days with the air filled with gleaming planes and the gentle sounds of spring blotted out by the roar of engines—these and others are the memories of those days. Our first shells fired by over-enthusiastic Canadians, what excitement and flurry they produced ! ! Last minute training ; last minute parties ; the brittle sense of imminent action ; suspense and, then, the 6th June, 1944. WE knew where we were ; the waiting was over, the endeavours of the last four years were to be put to the test.

INTO FRANCE

In the early hours of Tuesday, 13th June, 1944, the Battalion split itself in two. Very temporarily we thought, but it was to be nearly ten days before we were re-united. Shortly after breakfast on that morning, the marching part of the Battalion donned that most hated of all Army orders, Full Marching Order (F.M.O.), and marched away to STEYNING Station, thence by train to a transit camp at Hayward's Heath. None who were there will ever forget the days spent in that well-organised place—excellent food, Ritz service, and entertainment on a lavish scale. Not for many a day would they enjoy the like, and all took full advantage of what was offered. But even such a heaven as this had its moment of trial—ours fortunately was at the start, when by an error the route twixt station and camp was lengthened by the odd five miles—and the packs weighted, it would seem, by an extra fifty pounds ! !

But all good things end sometime and, on the 17th, the troops were taken down to Newhaven by Troop Carrying Vehicles (T.C.V.'s) and embarked in a U.S. and two U.K. Landing Craft Infantry (L.C.I.'s). Good weather favoured the voyage which was enlivened by experiments with a new, and useful, plaything—self-heating soup.

It was Derby Day, and some were disconcerted when " Happy Landing " came in a mere third—nor was it without omen, for next morning came disembarkation, and the majority had to wade ashore, chest-deep. We can all remember the impressive sight of all the shipping in the bay. We landed at COURSEULLES, and had a 14 mile march to our concentration area at VAUX-sur-SEULLES. There it was we dug our first slits in FRANCE, perhaps a little perfunctorily and with that rather hurt " scheme " feeling. We were still novices in the art and practice of war.

And now for the men there was little to do but wait for the rest of the Battalion, and the day of testing. For the officers, though, it was less of a holiday and the days were filled with " O " groups, plans, plans altered and new plans altogether.

Meanwhile, what of the Transport and its accompanying personnel ? It, too, had left in the very early hours of Tuesday, but its route was vastly different nor was it accomplished with such ease and speed. All that day we rolled through the lovely villages of Sussex and Surrey, and finally through the busy streets of London, and into a camp at Woodford, there to await the call to the boats. It wasn't until the 16th that the call came and away we went with high hopes to the loading quay of the East India docks, the crews in London buses—the only time they are likely to have a free ride in all history from L.P.T.B. And then a slow steam aboard our U.S. and U.K. Liberty ships to SOUTHEND where we lay off for the night. Saturday evening saw us off the shores of FRANCE and though the crossing had been perfect, the wind suddenly increased, lashed and harried the sea to such an extent that unloading was impracticable. Nor did it subside until another Friday had come, and we had spent a confined week aboard the boat. But it did calm and on the 23rd we transferred to a Landing Craft Tank (L.C.T.), and finally landed dry-shod in the early evening. How the hard-worked waterproofers cursed ! ! A quick run through the paved streets of COURSEULLES, de-waterproofing just outside, and then the few miles to VAUX and reunion with the remainder of the Battalion. The Unit was complete and ready for action.

INTO BATTLE

The time of action was now at hand and, after a Saturday and Sunday mainly devoted to last minute orders and preparations, we moved up in the early hours of Monday, 26th June. 44 Bde were to attack ST. MAUVIEU, 46 Bde the area round CHEUX, while 227 Bde were to go for TOURVILLE, GRAINVILLE and the crossings of the River ODON below these places. Our objective was GRAINVILLE. Most of Monday morning and early afternoon was spent amidst the mediums supporting the early attacks with a continuous cannonade ; it was our first immediate experience of the din of battle. As the afternoon wore on, we moved up to CHEUX and our start line south of LE HAUT DU BOSQ, an adjunct. When we reached CHEUX in the evening of 26th June, it was to find it far from clear ; many snipers still lurked in its shattered houses and its many treed orchards—nor was that all for, as the Battalion deployed towards the start line, tanks were encountered. By now it was dusk, nor was the light enhanced by a heavy downpour and that, mixed with the smoke and stench of battle and cattle, cast a sombre gloom over the whole area. Under these circumstances, it was decided to concentrate the Battalion in the southern outskirts of CHEUX and continue the advance in the morning. This was done and we dug in for the night. That day we suffered our first casualties—Lieut. John Bell was fatally wounded and Pte. Brophy of " A " Company was killed.

Next morning, 27th June, at 07.30 hours, we resumed the attack, but were held up by heavy mortar and M.G. fire from the start line. " B " Company had a bad time, and " D " passed through them. After an hour, " A " and " D " Companies were forward within 300 yards of the start line where there were a number of dug-in Tigers and Panthers. " C " Coy. went round by the right flank and though some elements succeeded in reaching the start line, they could not consolidate their gain. It was in this action that Major Stoker was wounded.

Meanwhile, some hundred yards back, four enemy tanks had succeeded in infiltrating into a farm within 150 yards of Bn. H.Q. They started to shell and, but for the quick spotting of Lieut. R. Bowers, 2nd i/c Anti-Tank Platoon, and the speedy action of Capt. A. N. Scott, his platoon commander, there might have been a different story to tell. Captain Scott, without regard for his own personal safety, brought two of his anti-tank guns into action at a range of 100 yards and succeeded in knocking out all four tanks after a hard battle. The coolness and accuracy of the gun crews was beyond praise and for their part, Capt. Scott gained the Military

Cross and L/Sgt. Oldale (later killed in action) the Military Medal. Cpl. Burgess, who had been particularly conspicuous with his gun, was killed in this action.

All the while the Battalion was being heavily mortared and casualties were heavy. No praise can be too great for the Stretcher Bearers (S.B.'s) whose work on that and for many days to come, was quite immense. For his great work, Sgt. R. Campbell, the Medical Sgt., won the Military Medal. Nor must we forget the jeep drivers and the carrier drivers from the mortar and carrier platoons who, following the fine example set by their Platoon Commanders, kept up a continuous evacuation under testing conditions. That night we buried our first dead, saw many refugees tired and weary pass through the shattered streets, and dug-in once again round CHEUX, while the 11th Armoured Division passed through to the river and the crossing that had been secured.

Next day, we moved in to the COLLEVILLE-MOUEN area and had a bloody battle in the dusk of evening at MOUEN. " A " Company, under Capt. Hay, had a field day and claimed 50 German dead as their share, but it was a precarious position and the Battalion spent an uncomfortable night around a MOUEN farm—they were tired and the men owed much to the restless energy of Colonel Young. Nor had the fight been without cost—we had lost 21 killed, including Lieuts. Armer and Harding of " D " Company and Lieut. Hilborn of " A " Company, the latter two being Canadian officers on loan to us. Major R. B. Maclachlan " D " Company was fatally wounded, while personally leading an attack in the face of enemy tank cross-fire which was enfilading his Company position. That evening, 28th June, the Q.M., Capt. A. Bain and four O.R.'s went missing after leaving the Battalion to rejoin " B " Echelon, presumably having taken a wrong turning and run into the enemy lines. All four O.R.'s were taken prisoner, but we were later sadly to learn that the Q.M. lost his life. From then on, " Q " matters were in the able hands of Lieut. F. I. M'Gilp, who was commissioned in the field.

Capt. Bain was the father of the Battalion. Having served throughout the war of 1914-18, he was a keen Territorial during the interval of peace. He was appointed Q.M. when the Battalion was formed, and his experience, enthusiasm and unique personality had been of inestimable value during the early mobilization, the prolonged period of training, and the subsequent mobilization for service overseas. The loss was most deeply felt by all ranks.

On the following day, 29th June, we relieved our sister Unit, the 2nd Glasgow Highlanders (H.L.I.) at COLLEVILLE, coming temporarily under command 46 (H.) Inf. Bde. It was on this day that the Germans staged their only major attempt to drive us back to the beaches and, though we missed the direct assault, we were subjected all day to heavy mortar and shell fire. Colonel Young and the 2nd i/c, Major Colwill, were both wounded, and Major R.

Sinclair of the 2nd Bn. Gordons assumed temporary command. After another noisy night, we moved to a wood south of MON-DRAINVILLE, on the 30th June. Not an ideal place for a Battalion, we did our best and in true 1815 style formed hollow square round a rather disgusting marsh. And here it was that our mortars first came into action on enemy posts on Hill 112, that famous enemy observation post over the ODON River. Nor were they too popular, for retaliation was prompt and the first " O " Group quickly disintegrated as 88's landed unpleasantly close. The enemy was counter-attacking strongly at GRAINVILLE on our right and once again we got the benefit of his mortars and guns. We had more casualties here, including Capt. Mundie, our R.A. observation officer, killed.

Next day, 1st July, representatives from the Royal Welch Fusiliers, who were to relieve us that night, came and, after another uncomfortable day, the relief was completed at 3 a.m. on Sunday morning, July 2nd.

Our first week of fighting was over, and we were out to rest and refit. We had learned much in a week. We had undergone that vital experience for all soldiers—the test under fire. And we had come out with colours flying and an enhanced reputation for our already famous regiment. Nor had it been without cost, for in that week we had lost 66 killed and 210 wounded.

INTERLUDE

It seemed quiet and, apart from the war-scarred environs, peaceful at NORREY-EN-BESSIN when we arrived that Sunday morning for rest and re-equipping. Both were much needed—the Battalion had lost 12 officers and 264 O.R.'s and much equipment had been rendered useless. And yet the choice of NORREY as a resting-place seems odd in retrospect—a glance at the situation map of that day will show the front line running north-south to BARON and East towards CAEN. We were at the tip of a salient with CARPIQUET aerodrome as its base. Nevertheless, we had a quiet period disturbed only by a two-day stay near ST. MAUVIEU where we came under command 32 Guards' Brigade during the Canadian attack on CARPIQUET. It was here that Colonel Young rejoined us, having refused to return to England, and right at the end that Major Ian MacKenzie, fresh from the classroom of the Staff College, came as our new Second-in-Command.

NORREY has pleasant memories for most—it was a rest and gave us our first contact with the French of whom the Duc will be best remembered. In a small way, we took part in the 14th July celebrations—two pipers, a detachment of " A " Company, Major Merrifield and the Padre were among the procession that honoured the village's dead in the last war and then honoured two British soldiers who had fallen nearby.

But big plans were in the making and another stern task awaited the Division—to make a feint attack towards EVRECY and draw off the enemy armour, while a major offensive was launched at CAEN. On the night 14th-15th July, the battalion, rested, re-equipped and almost at full strength, moved to an assembly area at HAUT DE VERSON on the banks of the River ODON.

Most of Saturday, 15th July, was spent at VERSON and final plans for the attack were made. There was much accurate shelling, most of it around Bn. H.Q., so that the Signal Platoon especially suffered casualties. In the early evening, the Battalion moved over the ODON to a forming-up point (F.U.P.) at GOURNAY where it spent a night of continuous shelling and mortaring, though, fortunately, without severe casualties. It was not a pleasant prelude for our attack on EVRECY at 05.30 hours next morning, 16th July.

At dawn on the 16th July, the move forward began but almost immediately our supporting tanks ran into a minefield. Furthermore, it was learned that the Battalions which had attacked earlier had failed to reach their objective and once again our start line was insecure. Without tank support and with enemy observation from Hill 112 covering the entire area of our advance, the Commanding Officer decided to consolidate in the open country beyond BARON and await a more favourable opportunity to continue the advance. But alas, Brigadier Mackintosh-Walker, who commanded 227 (H.) Infantry Brigade, and who had made a magnificent escape from Germany to Spain after being captured when with the 51st (H.) Division at ST. VALERY, in 1940, was killed at BARON. Control was temporarily lost, and so the Battalion remained in its position at BARON while Units of 53 Division went through. Meanwhile, heavy fire was encountered throughout Sunday and Monday, 16th and 17th July, and casualties increased. On the Sunday, night the German Air Force started bombing the area near " S " Company, though without loss to us. On Monday night, we were relieved and moved to LE HAUT DU BOSQ, the column being attacked from the air en route.

It had been a rather trying experience, and the casualties heavy considering the gains. All told, we had 76 casualties, the death of Major Palmer, who had taken over " C " Company a week before, being the most grievous. Colonel Young's wound proved more serious than it appeared, and he was ordered back to England by the Divisional Commander. In his place came Colonel Russell Morgan, of the Argylls, and he soon found a happy niche in our Unit. There was little to mark our stay here, except the atrocious weather, and apart from a little shelling and bombing of nearby gun positions, all was quiet.

THE BREAK-THROUGH

After a few days of rest, we moved across the front to CAUMONT on 23rd July and took over from the Americans during the night, 23rd-24th July, 1945, in positions in and around the town. It was the most forward point of the British line, and fighting there had temporarily reached stalemate. But not for long !!! The mortars had a field day with " Winifred " and " Jane," which were codesigns to call the fire of different groups of weapons, and sent over many hundreds of bombs. We also had our first real experience of active patrolling here, and it was here that we were joined by our new M.O., Capt. R. S. Sunderland, R.A.M.C., who was to serve the Battalion so efficiently until the end of the campaign. The Americans had established in CAUMONT a network of communications—30 miles of cable wire. This was taken over and greatly simplified by Capt. D. N. Steward, Signals Officer, who was shortly to become such an able I.O., and display the highest qualities as the Commanding Officer's right-hand man in many actions till the end of hostilities. On the 24th July, we were hit hard when the Carrier Officer, Capt. K. J. Ingram, most brilliant and well-beloved, was killed by a shell. His loss was most deeply felt by all.

Meanwhile on our right, the American advance from ST. LO was gaining momentum, and the hour for the bridgehead break-through was at hand. On Friday, night, 28th July, we were relieved by the K.O.S.B., and moved back to prepare for our part in the attack, of Sunday, 30th July. The Divisional objective was the high ground round ST. MARTIN DES BESACES and BOIS DU HOMMES. We were in the second wave, our objective being the vital cross-roads at HERVIEUX, midway between CAUMONT and ST. MARTIN.

Early on Sunday morning, 30th July, we moved up and were greatly heartened by the sight of many heavy bombers supporting our advance—it was our first direct air support. We reached our objective by mid-afternoon, and had the pleasure of seeing the armour stream through the breach which we had helped to make. The casualties had been light, but light as they were, we suffered a great loss by the death of C.S.M. Humble of " A " Company, whose conduct and leadership hitherto had been beyond praise. Much of the success of the operation was due to the excellent work of, and our co-operation with tanks of the 4th Battalion Coldstream Guards—our training with them in England bore full fruit.

The next few days were spent in expanding the corridor. There was little opposition and the brilliant weather gave it an almost peacetime aspect. It was not until we came to MONTCHARIVAL and AU CORNU, on the road to VASSY, on the 5th August, that we encountered any serious opposition. AU CORNU was fairly heavily shelled and we had casualties, including Major Hay wounded.

On Sunday, 6th August, the Gordons were to attack ESTRY, and we were to pass through them and take LE THEIL. But ESTRY was too strong a point, and the Battalion took over the attack after the Gordons had been pinned down. ESTRY, and a dozen other similar little villages at the Western end of the German salient that was to become the " FALAISE POCKET " had all the weapons of defence—machine gun nests, dug-in tanks, mortars and " call on " heavy artillery. Despite all this, by late evening of 6th August, the forward companies had reached the area of the church where resistance was strongest. Dark was fast falling and to avoid undue confusion, the Battalion, less " A " Company, was withdrawn to the north side of the VASSY road where it passed through the fringe of the village. " A " Company held a kind of outpost position in an orchard south of the road. It was utterly dark when we started digging—luckily, the soil was soft and, before long, all were under cover. Nor was it too soon for, about midnight, the enemy opened up with medium artillery and, with extraordinary accuracy, searched the orchards and fields where we were. By this time, the Gordons had joined us and a dual command was set up by Colonels Russell Morgan and Sinclair.

The village all that night, 6th/7th August, and next day and night, 7th/8th August, was a noisy, lively place—artillery exchanges, our own 3-in. mortars pounding the church area and the road itself covered by German Spandaus, and the crossroads by the M.M.G.'s and 88 of a dug-in Tiger Tank. Tribute must be paid to the excellent work of the Carrier platoon drivers who brought up food, and thrice daily ran the gauntlet along the precarious route from AU CORNU to ESTRY. In fact, throughout the first few weeks' fighting they had done the job again and again under very similar conditions. The battalion owed them a great debt.

On Monday it was learned that we were to be withdrawn so that the gunners could have a little elbow-room for firing and also for 44 (H.) Inf. Bde. to go through and clear the village. In the early hours of Tuesday, 8th August, some of " S " Company pulled out to rear H.Q. at AU CORNU where a counter-attack by three tanks and a Company of German infantry was beaten off by the A/Tk. R.A. and the Middlesex M.M.G.'s. Two tanks were destroyed. At 10.00 hours on Tuesday, Companies started to thin out and by 11.00 hours the area was almost clear. But by some mischance, there had been a misunderstanding about timings and our guns opened up in the area much sooner than expected— much to the annoyance of those members of Battalion H.Q. and

Support Company who still remained. The withdrawal, however, was effected without casualties and we took up a reserve position about a mile back.

The Battalion settled down here and, apart from some shelling and mortaring near the forward companies and a Spandau (never located) that fired occasional bursts at Bn. H.Q. and " S " Company area, all was quiet, comparatively speaking. The next few days were spent in recuperation and reinforcing our rather depleted ranks—patrols and a proposed " surrender " broadcast by a captured Pole were the only incidents to mark the passing of the days. On Saturday, 12th August, we came out of the line for a spell of much needed and well-earned rest. It was a day of great heat and Companies had to march 8 miles back to an area for the night —it was a very tired, almost exhausted, yet still cheerful battalion that dug its slits and settled down for its first full night's rest in a fortnight or more. Next morning saw us away back to our old haunts round CAEN. Despite the desolation of nearby MALTOT, these were happy, restful days by the ORNE. Every day the sun blazed overhead and it was refreshing to be able to plunge into the river and indulge in the carefree joys of a peacetime, now long forgotten. And each day the skies were filled with hurrying aircraft, sealing the doom of the German 7th Army. By the 18th August, the " FALAISE GAP " had been closed and what remained of the enemy outside the advancing wall of steely destruction, was in full retreat. The slogging, dreary days of the bridgehead were at an end and the open country of France lay before us—the chase was on ! ! !

Among the congratulatory messages received at the time were the following :—

From Army Commander on 2nd August, 1944.

" It was the 15th (Scottish) Division which broke through the enemy's main defence line South of CAUMONT on July 30th and opened the way for the Armoured Divisions to pass through.

The result of your great action on that day can now be seen by everyone.

You have set the very highest standard since the day you landed in Normandy, and I hope you are as proud of your achievements as I am to have you under my command.

(Signed) M. C. DEMPSEY."

From Corps Commander, 8th Corps, on 3rd August, 1944.

" I want again to congratulate you all on a magnificent achievement in the recent operations SOUTH of CAUMONT.

Your capture of the high ground in the area of the BOIS DU HOMME was vital to the success of the whole Second Army plan.

This was carried out in most difficult country and in the face of stiff enemy opposition. Furthermore, you held your ground against all enemy counter-attacks.

I am very glad to know how much the excellent co-operation between you and the 6th Guards Tank Brigade helped to make this operation such a success. It is a tribute to the training carried out between you, and has produced a state of mutual confidence, which will go far to ensure further successes in the future.

(Signed) R. N. O'CONNOR."

From Maj.-Gen. G. H. A. MacMillan, C.B.E., D.S.O., M.C., Comd. 15 (S.) Inf. Div., on 2nd August.

" I am indeed proud of the Division and I wish to include in my congratulations and thanks the 6 Guards Armoured Brigade whose splendid co-operation made our latest success possible."

(Signed) G. H. A. MacMILLAN."

From Maj.-Gen. C. M. Barber, D.S.O., Comd. 15 (S.) Inf. Div., on 23rd August.

" On assuming command of the 15th (Scottish) Division, I know I am expressing the feelings of all ranks in saying with what regret we learned that Maj.-Gen. G. H. A. MacMillan, C.B.E., D.S.O., M.C., had been wounded. I am glad to be able to tell you that his wound is not serious and, on your behalf, I wish him a speedy recovery.

It was as much due to his inspiring leadership as to your fine fighting qualities that the Division has earned the great reputation it now holds.

I assume command with a great sense of pride and of the honour done me, and with your help I shall endeavour to maintain our reputation.

(Signed) C. M. BARBER."

THE ELUSIVE FOX

After weeks of positional warfare round CAEN and then FALAISE, the front had become fluid and, with this change, there came an element of confusion. And so for the first few days our advance was made in small bounds—BOIS HALBOUT, near FALAISE, on the 18th August, through FALAISE on the 23rd August, through TRUN the next day and then on the 25th, the triumphal march across NORMANDY to LOUVIERS and the River SEINE.

Around FALAISE and TRUN we saw in detail the destruction of an army—it was carnage on a gigantic scale. Along every road and in every field and orchard lay tanks, vehicles, horses, guns and men of a defeated and demoralised army. And we realised to the full what we owed to those glinting, silver planes that had roared above us as we sported in the waters of the ORNE. Never again until we reached the frontiers of GERMANY would we have to face the ordeals of CHEUX, COLLEVILLE, MONDRAIN-VILLE, BARON or ESTRY—the planes had reaped a rich harvest and it was up to us to use it to full advantage.

On the 25th August, we thrust across to EMANVILLE and what a wonderful day it was. Beyond TRUN, the destruction disappeared and, instead of the overpowering stench of dead horses and men, we breathed sweet clean air and our eyes were enchanted by vistas of lovely country untouched by the foul fingers of war. And what a welcome we had ! ! At every little hamlet, at each crossroads, the people came with flowers and flags, fruit and wine to greet us, and cheers and happy smiles to speed us on our way. This was the day we had fought so hard to see—the genuine joy, the rapture of these liberated people was tremendous reward for the hard days that had gone before. And so it was all the way to EMANVILLE and again next day when we entered LOUVIERS, a sizeable town with all its inhabitants in joyful mood to greet their liberators. It was a really tremendous tonic and we all felt re-vitalised and ready for whatever was before us. It was at LOUVIERS too, that we found a new slogan, another battle-cry to replace the rather worn and out-moded " stretcher bearer " shout of bygone days—" Cigarette pour Papa " was a French phrase, albeit slang, that every Jock soon learned and understood to the detriment of his tobacco stocks. When children of 9 and 10 smoke, and you are in a country of large families and little tobacco, the demand is bound to be great ! ! ! But it was all part of the game, and few were refused.

OVER THE SEINE

Often in peacetime memories we had crossed rivers—but never had they equalled the SEINE in size, nor had there been opposition on the other bank. The Division was to force a crossing in the loop of the river EAST of LOUVIERS, while 43rd Division on our right and the Canadians on our left crossed at VERNON and in the ROUEN area respectively. The Gordons and H.L.I. were to make the initial crossings and the battalion's first task was to secure an undestroyed bridge that spanned the river between a little island in midstream and the opposite bank. To do this, a platoon of " C " Company under Lieut. D. Graham was sent ahead, with the remainder following closely behind. The crossing started in the early evening and, by dusk the major portion of the battalion was over and our bridgehead secured. For his part in this action, Sgt. P. Daly, M.M., of " A " Company, was awarded the D.C.M. Our casualties were extremely light and, in this connection, we were more fortunate than the Gordons. Their first three boats had been sunk with heavy losses, and the first of their men to get ashore had been captured. Most of these latter were, however, released when a platoon of " B " Company attacked their captors.

All that night, 27th/28th August, and throughout the dark hours of early morning the Sappers worked a ferry from ST. PIERRE de VAUVRAY and by midday on the 28th August, the Battalion and its transport was almost complete and ready to start enlarging the area held. In conjunction with the rest of the Brigade, we moved forward that afternoon, clearing a large tract of woodland on our way. In the evening we were ordered to advance and take a commanding feature above CONNELLES, a village at the western end of the river loop. This was effected without incident and by midnight we were firmly established there, with 44 (L.) Inf. Bde. passing through to even further objectives. And there we stayed amidst a continuous and heavy downpour, all the 30th and the morning of the 31st August. About midday, we moved down into CONNELLES and there found shelter and a warm welcome from the inhabitants.

It was during our few days here that Lieut.-Colonel Russell Morgan left us to assume command of his old Argyll battalion—he had won a place in our affection and respect and we were sorry to see him go. Yet he was still in the Brigade and, often in the days to come, we were to see him and work with him again. We were glad to welcome Lieut.-Colonel H. P. Mackley, O.B.E., of the Cameronians, who had returned from an appointment in Italy.

INTO BELGIUM

On the 3rd September, we moved to a little place called LE TRONQUAY, North of Lyon-la-Foret, spent a night there and then moved on to GAILLESFONTAINE, near Forges Les Eaux. Another day there and on the 5th September we moved across the Somme to Conchy sur Canche, S.W. of ST. POL. These were quiet, uneventful journeys except for a little shooting round the Somme bridge. Troop transport was the difficulty at this time and the move to Conchy had been made by " S " and " H.Q." Companies only. It was to be another full day before the infantry companies arrived. But we were ready to move on the morning of the 7th September, and we set off on the long journey through North France to Belgium. What a day and night that was—we had known welcomes before but nothing could compare with what we were to meet during the hours of that journey. We passed through LILLE in the early evening and pandemonium broke out—great crowds lined the streets and flooded round the vehicles whenever we stopped. Hands were limp with being shaken—motor-cyclists and jeep travellers, being more easily got hold of, were removed from their vehicles and feted. Nor was this the zenith of our welcome—Belgium lay ahead and we were told that it would outdo anything yet experienced. And so it did! Originally we were to have gone to COURTRAI by way of MENIN, but that was altered en route and we skirted TOURCOING and ROUBAIX to cross the border at MOUSCRON. We arrived there in the dark—but on this night there was no holding the people! Lights shone brilliantly everywhere—every shop window, every house was ablaze. It was Christmas and Carnival on an unprecedented scale. There was no blackout for as the locals said, with the simple logic of joy, there were no German planes left. We were a little sceptical on that point! But that was a night beyond description, an experience that will live forever with those who were part of it. Yet wonderful as it was, it came as a great relief when we hit the open country again and harboured for the night at the little village of HELCHIN. " O " group at 02.00 hours, 8th September, and a little sleep before an early advance-to-contact move towards the LYS river near GHENT.

" A " company went to DEURLE, " C " to GHENT, with Bn. H.Q. and " B " company at St. Martin's, LAETHEM. What delightful places these were, and what pleasant memories there are for all who were at them. Even GHENT, then a battleground, had its reminders and souvenirs of happiness, and that joy which is such an integral part of life amidst happy families. There the Pipe Major and his " gallants " had one of the finest receptions of their tour. The Belgiums were wild with delight, and the Kilts and Pipes took a winning trick. And there we stayed, with the odd countermanded movement order—life was full of them these days !—to disturb the even tenor of our ways, until the 11th Sept., when we moved to HUMBECK, north of BRUSSELS. It was quiet there, too, and many of the battalion were able to go into the capital for a few hours on the 12th September and sample the joys of an almost peacetime city, so quickly had it returned to its former ways of life. The others, less fortunate, saw a local Belgium team beat the battalion by 3 goals to 2.

Next day, the 13th September, saw us on the move again and in a significant direction — North-east towards the Belgo-Dutch frontier. By midday, we were across the Albert Canal where the Durham Light Infantry had fought so hard. 44 Bde. had taken the bridgehead over and, after we had passed through them we were in the vanguard once again and in hot pursuit of the Germans retreating to the line of the Escaut-Meuse Canal. As we covered the miles between the two waterways, we were met by rapturous people with tales of Germans clearing out but a short time before. Through delirious MEERSHAUT we went to the outskirts of MOL, where the scene became a little more warlike and the battalion deployed to clear the town. The Recce had reported scattered opposition and had one of their armoured cars knocked out. But the enemy was not in the mood for effective resistance and after an artillery " stonk," the infantry moved forward to clear the houses, while Capt. Scott moved down the main street in his carrier to receive the plaudits and rapturous thanks of a delighted populace ! There are touches of comedy even in war. We soon found that the town had been evacuated and while we consolidated the approaches, the Argylls, carried on Sherman tanks, raced through to try and take the Donck bridge over the Escaut intact. Alas, they were too late—the bridge had been blown.

We settled down in MOL, Bn. H.Q. being in a former Nazi barracks. That night, 13th September, we were feted by the locals, and the Jocks smoked as many cigars and had as much wine as they liked. Next day, 14th September, was fairly uneventful except for two rather sharp and unexpected bouts of shelling that found Bn. H.Q. with great accuracy. There were, however, no casualties. Next day, too, was uneventful, except for the presentation of medals to Officers and men of the Division by Field-Marshal Montgomery, and for preparations to force a crossing of the canal near DONCK next morning.

The following is an extract of Field-Marshal Montgomery's address to those of the Division who attended the presentation :—

" In the present operations we have employed some divisions that had already done a great deal of fighting, and were very experienced. There were others with no experience at all. The divisions without any experience have made very good use of their training.

They have done every bit as well as the old stagers, and I can say that THERE IS NO ONE TO BEAT THE 15TH (SCOTTISH) DIVISION TO-DAY.

I hope that all units will get to know what I have said about the Division. I hope, too, that this news will get home to SCOTLAND (although I know that you have some Englishmen with you, and that is a good thing), and that you will tell your folk at home that I came here to-day and told you THAT THE 15TH SCOTTISH DIVISION HAD DONE MAGNIFICENTLY."

In the early hours of the 16th September, we moved up to a concentration area and there awaited many hours for the Gordons to form the bridgehead which we were to pass through and expand. The Gordons were pinned down by heavy fire, and as 44 Brigade had already secured a limited bridgehead north of GHEEL, our venture was abandoned and back we came to MOL. But shortly after our return, the order came to move again and off we went to an area N.E. of GHEEL. We were there to recce and tape crossings east of the established bridgehead for a further series of crossings on a wide front. On the afternoon of the 17th Sept., Sunday, the Dakotas and gliders carrying airborne troops who were to establish the NIJMEGEN salient passed overhead. It was a really magnificent spectacle.

We spent the whole of the 17th September recceing and taping crossings and also covering an area of the southern canal bank with the Carrier platoon. On the 18th September, we were relieved by the Seaforths and went into Brigade reserve at GHEEL. 44 Brigade had had a very bad time in their bridgehead and the Gordons and Argylls were called in to relieve them. That night we had good billets and, all would have been well, but for a major tragedy. During the night, three heavy shells hit " A " Company's billet—a school—and every Sergeant was killed or wounded. Sgt. Davidson's death from his wounds was particularly felt—he had proved himself a magnificent leader and had always been an inspiration to the men around him.

Most of the next day, 19th September, was spent in GHEEL, but in the early evening we moved up to a wood just short of the canal, preparatory to crossing and expanding the bridgehead. The enemy had several self-propelled (S.P.) guns over the other side and directed much accurate fire on the Battalion concentration area. But we were well dug-in and nobody was hurt. The crossing was quiet and quite uneventful. The attack was more or less successful, though " B " Company and the Carrier platoon (on foot) pushed too far on and ran into very strong positions. The Carriers and an Anti-Tank section along with " B " Company had heavy casualties, the most felt being Capt. E. Agnew and Sgt. Mack of the Carriers, who were badly wounded and refused to hamper the withdrawal of the rest of their men to a more secure position.

All the next day, 20th September, the bridgehead was heavily shelled and mortared, but remained perfectly secure. That night, however, in accordance with higher strategy, the Brigade was withdrawn to the south of the canal. " A " Company remained forward to cover the road into GHEEL while the remainder of the Battalion returned to GHEEL.

The following extract from a Sitrep of 16th September, 1944, by the German I Para. Army, is interesting :—

" LOCK MACHINERY AT WINEGHEN BLOWN BY 719 INF. DIV. INDECISIVE FIGHTING IN THE AART BRIDGEHEAD. THE 15TH (SCOTTISH) INFANTRY DIVISION IDENTIFIED IN THIS AREA FIGHTS TOUGHLY AND STUBBORNLY."

INTO HOLLAND

Next day, 22nd September, the remainder of the Brigade moved into HOLLAND, while we stayed under command of 7th Armoured Division to help hold the canal area. That evening the Bn. moved up to its new positions and much patrolling of the southern bank occupied the night. That night the enemy withdrew and the bitterly contested battlefield of the GHEEL bridgehead, with its dead and barren destruction, was ours for the taking. It had been a hard, unpleasant battle and losses by the two Brigades high, but once again our sacrifice had not been in vain. Our resistance had tied down strong forces needed more urgently elsewhere and 30 Corps had been enabled to force a quick canal crossing further west and start its dramatic drive to EINDHOVEN, NIJMEGEN and ARNHEM and thence, we hoped, to the very heart of industrial Germany in the Ruhr. It was yet another notable achievement and added to our laurels, ever green and ever growing in stature and quality.

The following message was received from the Divisional Comd., Maj.-General C. M. Barber, D.S.O. :—

" I am most pleased to be able to send you the following extract from a letter received from the Corps Commander, 12 Corps :—

" The reason that 30 Corps were able to break out so quickly from their bridgehead was due largely to the fact that a great proportion of the enemy's reserves in that part of the theatre of operation were drawn against the 15th (Scottish) Division bridgehead north of GHEEL. The 15th (Scottish) Division has had some very tough fighting and has, as well, suffered many casualties. It is a small consolation—but the initial success of 30 Corps does owe a lot to what the 15th (Scottish) Division has achieved."

I wish my best congratulations given to all those concerned in meriting the above tribute for their toughness and stout hearts during the unpleasant time they had north of GHEEL."

On the 23rd September, we were relieved and moved to rejoin the Brigade at EINDHOVEN. Shortly before six that evening, we crossed into HOLLAND, and there lay but one more frontier before our task was at an end. We reached the town in complete darkness and parked in the road. Our welcome was more restrained and lacked the ebullience of the Belgians, but none the less it was warm and most sincere. As an indication of this, within half-an-hour of our arrival, every man had a bed and a house in which to sleep—it was hospitality on a scale never before experienced. Next day was spent in EINDHOVEN, too, and the rest and comfort were much appreciated. Services were held in the local Baptist Church that day, Sunday, 24th September, and it was refreshing to have civilians in the congregation, even if their Dutch words blended a little strangely with the English of our hymns. Early next morning, Monday, 25th September, we moved to a concentration area just east of BEST. The Gordons were to secure a start line west of the town, while we and the Argylls, were to go through and clear NASTE BEST. The Gordons, however, ran into severe opposition, suffered heavy casualties, and fresh plans were hatched. Most of the trouble had been caused by a large butter factory, converted into an enemy strongpoint. It had been the Mortar Officer's main target for our attack and it was with somewhat mixed feelings that he saw it disappearing under the rockets of some obliging Typhoons. The battalion stayed that night in the concentration area—a rather miserable, wet and burnt-out wood. Next morning, 26th September, we moved N.E. of BEST to clear a large wooded area south of the small village of LEIMDE. In conjunction with the Argylls, we beat through the area and though there was a good amount of resistance, the Battalion did well and by the end of the day had taken nearly eighty prisoners. The Argylls on our left had had a more difficult time and, just before dusk, it was decided to withdraw to positions a little south of the wooded zone. Our casualties had been fairly light though we lost two of our Canadian officers, Capt. M'Cabe and Lieut. Graham, both of " C " Coy, and both wounded.

Lieut. Struck, another of our Canadian officers, had a notable exploit that afternoon. He and about five of his platoon were crawling up a ditch when, on looking round, they saw a similar party of Germans emulating them some little distance in rear. Lieut. Struck's party rapidly changed direction, only to run into a party of thirty-five enemy. Just at that rather critical moment, the gunners put down the red smoke indication for the Typhoons and down the roaring, shrieking, rending rockets came. The rockets done and the cannon fire finished, Lieut. Struck and his Bren Gunner stood up, fired a burst with the gun and, with commendable promptness and docility, a German officer and thirty-four of his men advanced, with upstretched hands ! !

The rest of the night and the rest of the next day was spent in comparative quiet. There was, however, active patrolling and a few prisoners were taken. Division, meanwhile, had formed the opinion that our immediate opponents were in the mood for surrender, given a little encouragement by rocket Typhoons. And so on the 28th, a loud-speaker van was brought up and installed behind a farm less than 300 yards from the enemy outposts. A short harangue, red smoke and the weird thunder of Typhoons ! A patrol was sent out and brought in a handful of the enemy. A couple of hours later the process was repeated, but this time without tangible result. That night, 28th September, 44 (L.) Brigade on our right repelled a vicious counter-attack with heavy losses and at the same time there was a report of large infantry forces moving in our direction. Furious fire was brought down by the gunners, 4.2-in. mortars and our own 3-in. mortars. Nothing more was heard of the enemy force and no attack materialised. Next day was quiet too, except for patrolling, and artillery and mortar exchanges. It was not hard fighting, nor were casualties heavy, but it demanded a high degree of continuous alertness, which proved extremely tiring. Next day, 30th September, we were relieved by the 1st Gordons of 51 (Highland) Division which had come into 2nd Army. By late evening, the relief was complete, and we set off to the BAKEL area for a period of training and rest.

And so we arrived at the little village of MILHEEZE in the early hours of Monday morning, 1st October, and installed ourselves in the billets that had been arranged for us. We didn't know how long our stay was to be, but there was a minimum break of five days. The first two were spent in cleaning up and then we got down to some training. Blanco and drill parades re-asserted themselves and generally an atmosphere of peacetime prevailed. But this illusion, though, was rather rudely shattered when a few nights after our arrival, two jeeps were blown up on mines placed across a road in our area by some German patrol. This event roused not a little interest and, on further investigation, it was discovered that the enemy was dug-in about two miles from " S " Coy., and that the area we were using for training was a no-man's land under German observation. Shades of Shaw and Gilbert ! ! Guards were increased, patrols instituted, but even so our life was not materially changed. Training continued, the Divisional Commander took the salute at a march past on Sunday, 8th October, there were still cinema shows at DEURNE and ENSA concerts at GEMERT. We are generally recognised as a phlegmatic race—I suppose this was just another example of the truth of that belief ! !

The days passed evenly and quietly. There were, of course, the usual flaps—a Corps attack on the REICHSWALD FOREST area which was cancelled and another—very secret—that was on, then off, then on again. A military round-about that made your head whirl ! ! !

On Thursday, 19th October, the MILHEEZE chapter closed and we returned whence we had come nearly three weeks before to the dripping, deceptive woods of DONDERDONCK and VLEUT. Nothing had altered since our last sojourn there, except that trenches which had been dry and reasonably comfortable were now miniature pools and the mud had become more consistent and evident everywhere. But our stay was to be of short duration— big things were about to happen and, within a few days, the 2nd Army was to surge forward again and the whole of S.W. HOLLAND up to the River MAAS cleared of the enemy. Even as we relieved the 1st Gordons, units of 53 (Inf.) Division were opening their assault on S' HERTOGENBOSCH, the preliminary move of the whole operation. 51st (H.) Division was concentrating for a drive in the centre towards BOXTEL and beyond. This took place two days after the relief, on the 21st October, and our part in the pattern of attack was almost ready to be played.

The five days at DONDERDONCK were fairly quiet ones and followed very nearly the style of our former stay—artillery and mortar exchanges with a 10 to 1 advantage to us, night patrolling and all the other routine of defence. Casualties were light, though the death of Cpl. Phillips, from shell fire, was a sad loss. During the peace time years of training in England, he had been employed solely in the Officers' Mess, and we had greatly admired him for the facility with which he had adapted himself, quickly and efficiently, to the arduous work of an Infantry Section Leader.

Meanwhile, plans for the advance were completed and we were to attack towards the BEST-BOXTEL road on the 25th October. But a patrol on the night 23rd/24th October found empty positions and silence wherever they went—the enemy had flown under cover of darkness. And so the advance was put forward and, at mid-day on the 24th October, we moved forward to our preliminary objective on the BEST road. There was no opposition, though the frequent ditches and deep mud made the passage of our small M.T. column difficult. A few mines were encountered but in this respect we were more fortunate than the two flanking battalions who ran into large belts of mines and booby traps. The two forward Companies—" A " and " C "—moved forward and consolidated on the line of the railway. An uneventful night passed, and next morning we moved again to an area round the little village of NOTEL, near OIRSCHOT, which had been occupied by 44 (L.) Brigade the previous night. Meanwhile, reports were circulating of our Recce on the outskirts of TILBURG—no one was quite clear what the position really was, but at least we now knew that the next immediate objective was TILBURG. On Thursday, 26th October, we left NOTEL and moved to a concentration area at MOERGESTEL, preparatory to a proposed attack on GOIRLE, five miles S.W. of TILBURG. The attack, however, was not needed and next day, 27th October, after 44 (L.) Brigade had had a small skirmish in the eastern outskirts, TILBURG was ours and the marching troops of the Battalion entered in the early afternoon of Friday, 27th October. The bridges of the WILHELMINA Canal had, however, been blown and it wasn't until after dark that the tracked and wheeled part of the Battalion could enter the town. We received another tremendous welcome with comfortable billets for the night as the greatest prize—the Anti-Tank Platoon indulging in the truly regal splendour of King William II's Palace.

There were halcyon visions of garrison duties here, but they were soon cast aside. A serious threat had developed at the eastern base of our Dutch salient—two German Panzer divisions were attacking from the DEURNE Canal, at MEIJEL, and were threatening the little town of ASTEN. The American Armoured Division there was too weak on the ground to hold them and so we were hurriedly despatched to stem the tide and push the enemy back. The Battalion left TILBURG in the late afternoon of Saturday, 28th October, and reached a concentration area at LAARBROEK, a little hamlet just north of ASTEN, in the early hours of Sunday morning, 29th October. After a few hours rest, we moved into ASTEN and took up positions covering the southern approaches of the town. This, however, was but a temporary expedient and at dusk we moved forward to an area beyond HEUSDEN, where we relieved the Americans.

" B " and " C " Companies were astride the main road and forward into a wood, which covered a large area right of the road —" A " Company were in rear of it. The area of the wood and the farms round it had been well registered by enemy medium guns and the shelling at times was very intense. During Sunday night, several enemy succeeded in infiltrating from the south into the wood but were taken prisoner by a platoon of " A " Company that beat through the wood at first light on Monday, 29th October. Apart from shelling and mortaring, Monday was comparatively quiet, but once again that night the enemy attacked the wood. One party was quickly dealt with by a platoon of " A " Company under 2nd/Lt. A. Healey, who had been moved to a position south of the wood. They held their fire until the enemy was but 30 yards away—not one escaped. Meanwhile, others had again infiltrated into the wood and succeeded in capturing Sgt. W. Chapman and Cpl. W. Hartley of the Signal Platoon, who were repairing damaged lines at the time. The Commanding Officer had called down the entire Divisional artillery on the wood and, in the resultant confusion, Sgt. Chapman made good his escape. As he ran a stick grenade was thrown and he received multiple wounds of a serious nature— yet he made the 500 yards to Anti-Tank Platoon H.Q. unaided. A notable achievement.

After his second defeat round the wood, the enemy gave up his attempts to reach it and for the last few days of our stay, life was uneventful. Positions were improved and the Companies moved forward about one mile against no opposition. Meanwhile, 44 (L.) Brigade had driven the enemy from LIESEL and had advanced to within a mile of MEIJEL, but were stopped by mine-fields and heavy artillery fire. On Monday, 6th November, the 6th Royal Scots Fusiliers (R.S.F.), who had had casualties over in the MEIJEL area came to relieve us, and we moved back into billets at ASTEN. There we stayed for thirty-six hours, until the 8th November, when we moved over to the MOOSTDIJK—NEER-KANT—SCHEIM area, north of MEIJEL, and relieved the King's Own Scottish Borderers (K.O.S.B.) and Royal Scots. Another comparatively uneventful forty-eight hours there and then back to ASTEN, on 10th November, for another three days in billets.

The three day's rest ended on Monday, 13th November, when we moved up to our old area, forward of the much disputed wood, and relieved the R.S.F.

It was a quiet, uneventful take-over, for by now the enemy had withdrawn from our immediate front and there was some doubt as to whether there was anything to bar our way to MEIJEL except mines and road blocks. Patrols there were though in plenty, and our rather peaceful quiet was broken at 4 p.m. on Tuesday, 14th November, when the 51st (H.) Division, on our right, opened their attack with a tremendous barrage from massed artillery. That night, 14th/15th November, a Platoon of " C " Company, under Lieut. S. S. Drew, went into MEIJEL and apart from a few small posts on the eastern outskirts, they found it deserted. They took up positions round the ruined church, remained there throughout the night awaiting the arrival of the Battalion next morning. And so it happened that next day, 15th November, slowly and methodically, Companies moved forward and took over MEIJEL and the little village of DONK to the south. But the retreating Germans had done their job of demolition and mine-laying well— great numbers of trees had been felled across the road, craters had been blown, and all roads, tracks, verges, and possible vehicle pull-ins, had been liberally strewn with mines of all types—" S," Teller, " R " mines, and the new and unpleasant Schumine. But the Engineers and our own Pioneers did a great job and our casualties were very slight—the Scout car, one of the Anti-Tank platoon 15-cwt. trucks, and about three men wounded on Schumines. The civilians, who had remained in MEIJEL, too, rendered us valuable assistance—they knew where most of the mines had been placed and either marked them or told us where they had been put.

Gradually the place was cleared up, wide roads cut through the rubble, and a bridge constructed over the canal south of DONK. Life of a sort returned to MEIJEL. There was intermittent shelling, much patrolling up to the DEURNE Canal, and great activity by our 3-in. mortars.

After nearly four days in MEIJEL we pushed forward to the canal and " B " Company linked up with tanks of 4th Armoured Brigade who had come from BERINGEN, a village about a mile east of the canal. The Sappers quickly bulldozed a causeway into the canal by the blown bridge and on the night of the 19th November, the Battalion moved over the canal and took over BERINGEN. All was quiet there, apart from a brief but sharp period of shelling soon after our arrival. The inevitable rain was falling and fires still burned fitfully in the area—a dreary scene.

Next day, 20th November, the Gordons passed through us, closely followed by the Argylls, while we stayed put. There had been talk of moving that day, and all the next we stood by ready to push on, but as darkness fell for our third night in Beringen, we got the stand-down ! Next morning, 22nd November, however, we did move—at least as freely as the mud would allow ! ! Our way lay across country, over tracks that were scarcely discernible and knee-deep in thick, glutinous, treacherous mud. And all this under a leaden sky, distributing its rain with ample generosity and great effect ! Fortunately, perhaps, for us the enemy had withdrawn and we had only to contend with the weather and terrain. It was quite enough ! But somehow we made it and reached the hamlet of BROEK, where we harboured for the night. A little shelling, most of it some distance away, was all we could report in the way of enemy activity.

On the 23rd November, we resumed the vanguard role and pushed through the other two Battalions to the town of HORST. Again there was no opposition and the only hindrances were a few mines, road craters, tree blocks, foul weather and the mud. We consolidated HORST, linked up with the infantry of 11 Armoured Division who had been coming down on our left and then pushed a Company forward to secure an important crossroads north of the town. The only real battle in HORST was a purely internal one between Brigade H.Q. and ourselves over houses and H.Q. sites— the Brigadier was slightly ruffled when he found a house he wanted marked " Mortars H.Q. 67." As ever, of course, the side with the greater material advantages won ! HORST was quiet apart from a little shelling—a 4.2-in. mortar truck was hit and the night made lively by its exploding bombs !

Next day, 24th November, was spent in HORST, but on the 25th, again in the van, we moved to EIKELEMBOSCH, when the Argylls and Gordons passed through to TIENRAY and its environs. A night there and then next morning, 26th November, we moved off again with BLITTERSWIJK on the River MAAS as our objective. The little village of MEGELSUM, a mile or so short of the objective was secured soon after mid-day, and there one Company and Bn. H.Q. established themselves. Meanwhile, " C " Company pushed on to BLITTERSWIJK, and with the help of our Scots Guards Churchills soon overcame some slight opposition and got into the village. " B " Company then moved up and we held the area quite firmly. Shelling was fairly heavy in the village, but casualties almost non-existent, though Bn. H.Q. in MEGELSUM had a narrow escape when three shells landed very close, one actually hitting the house. All next day, 27th November, active patrolling went on and unearthed a little pocket west of BLITTERSWIJK— this we were going to deal with in the afternoon, when suddenly, and most unexpectedly, a Battalion of Royal Ulster Rifles from 3 (Br.) Division appeared to relieve us. The Commanding Officer was loath to hand over our rather untidy area, but it had to be, and by late evening we had handed over and were on our way to billets and rest in the now familiar environs of ASTEN.

The preceding month had been a testing one. Little rest, foul weather, the bleak countryside, the terrible rash of mines that marred the roads, fields and tracks, the inevitable mud and the constant need for alertness ; all these had made it an arduous, if not startlingly adventurous, time. But tired as we were, we came back with the happy knowledge that once again we had done a good job, quickly and with small loss under the worst conditions. It was indeed a pleasure to return to ASTEN for the few precious days of rest, and in its peaceful air, to see the full fruits of our endeavours. For, when first we came, it had been directly menaced, fearful and full of frightened people—now it was a quiet backwater and the flood and fury of battle had ebbed away many miles to the east.

And so for the next eight days we relaxed, found peace in undisturbed sleep, amusement at the ASTEN ASTORIA and other luxurious local cinemas, and found a little comfort in the homes and around the fires of our Dutch hosts. The Pipe Band played, St. Andrew's Day was celebrated by us, while the " locals " observed the Feast of St. Nicholas a week later in somewhat quieter strain ! Christmas was fast approaching and rumours of " Home " leave became a fact. Spirits were high and the recent discomforts an almost dim shadow of the past.

WINTER ON THE MAAS

Midway through our rest we learned that 44 (L.) Brigade had taken BLERICK and thus eliminated all resistance west of the MAAS, and it appeared that for some little time to come, we would have a holding role along the banks of that broad stream. And so it was that on Thursday, 7th December, we left for BAARLO, and took over a section of the river line from two Welsh Battalions of 53 Inf. Division. There we stayed for almost fourteen days—observing, patrolling, keeping constant watch. It was no period of incident or great excitement, nor yet was it dull. Our opponents over the water were from a Parachute Division and not infrequently crossed the river in small parties, lying up by day and ambushing our own patrols by night. Nor was this difficult for the front was thinly held. Cover on our side was plentiful and mist often hung heavily over the river and its steep banks. There were a fair number of artillery and mortar exchanges ; spandau and sniper fire often broke the still hush. On several days German fighters flew over the area, telephone wires were cut, reports of enemy and agents with wireless sets were not infrequent and there was always the Baron at Bn. H.Q.—a character with Phillips Oppenheim possibilities and always a fruitful source of surmise and conjecture. All in all, BAARLO was a strangely interesting yet eerie place, and if the days there were lacking in excitement, there was sufficient incident to occupy the thoughts and interest the mind.

On 13th December, Field Marshal Montgomery presented officers and men of the Division with medal ribbons. The following is an extract from his speech to those on parade :—

" I remember very clearly visiting your Division in England when I came back from ITALY, and I well remember your Division landing in NORMANDY when you came over just after D-day. You were untried then, though you had some veterans with you. I remember the first time your Division went into battle at the River ODON, and I remember feeling anxious that the Division should acquit itself well. One can't help feeling anxious at these times, though there is no need to. Your Division did very well indeed, and you have never looked back since. You have only to look at the Battle Honours on the stage behind me—I have noticed well known names like CAUMONT—to realise how much you have done.

I expect that to-day there are representatives here of every Unit in the Division. When you go back, I would like you to tell the others that I came here to-day, and that I think this Division has done awfully well. In this fighting, no Division has done better, and it is a first class show. We did not expect anything else, but it is very creditable for all that."

Possibly, though, the highlight of the whole period was the U.K. leave ballot on December 16th—there were separate draws for Officers, Warrant Officers and Sergeants, and the remaining Other Ranks. It may be of interest to record that Capt. R. T. Johnston, Sgt. W. Newton, and Pte. W. Evans (A.C.C.), were the first out of the hat in their respective draws.

On the 20th December, we were relieved by the Argylls and went into Brigade reserve near HELDEN. We had hoped to have Christmas out of the immediate line but in this we were unfortunate and, after three quiet days, we moved up to the KESSEL sector and relieved the Gordons on Christmas Eve. Christmas Day, itself, was much like any other—the only reminder being a mince pie per man supplied by our thoughtful Quartermaster ! !

And so the festive season passed, with little to show for its passage. Days were much the same as at BAARLO, though this time the night's still air was shattered by the ugly crunch of our Battalion mortars. All night and every night, they plugged away doing anything from silencing German carol singers on Christmas Eve to giving a Brock's benefit to bring in the New Year. There were the usual patrol scares and, from time to time, actual enemy did appear and in one neat operation cut off and captured four of our men in a forward post. The first U.K. leave parties left for home on New Year's Eve, and on the 2nd January, 1945, the Battalion was relieved by the Argylls and went back into Brigade reserve at HELDEN. Here we held rather belated Christmas and New Year festivities—and for the first time in months, the Jocks had some real English beer, if only a little !

Despite the dinners and festive food, the five days at HELDEN were by no means quiet peaceful ones—in fact, it was generally felt that, to be in reserve, was far more tedious and tiring than being in the line—nor was there the consolation of the nightly rum ! On the 7th January, 1945, we relieved the Gordons in familiar BAARLO, unchanged in appearance or character since our last tenure except for the absence of the notorious Baron and his dubious entourage, evacuated by the Argylls. Again there is the same story to tell of cold vigils, and wearisome nights, heavy snow and icy, treacherous roads. And so the days passed slowly with little to show for it all, though on the 13th January, the village was fairly heavily shelled and Sgt. Fisher, the Stretcher-Bearer Sergeant was killed. On the 15th January, a party of the Royal Air Force came to stay with us for a few days and see themselves how the Army, whom they so excellently supported, live when in contact with the enemy. Four days later, 19th January, we were invaded by green berets and we heard that a Commando Brigade was to relieve us, while we in turn relieved 44 (L.) Infantry Brigade in the BLERICK Sector. The relief was completed by the night of the

21st January, and the Battalion found itself in reserve and split in two—half at MAASBREE and the other at SEVENUM. Under command came a company of DUTCH patriots, with the Mortar Officer officially acting as LO but, in fact, doing the work of a rather harassed C.Q.M.S., and M.T. Corporal, combined !

Our stay here was brevity itself for within two days of esconcing ourselves, we suffered another invasion—this time by red berets—and we learned that 6th Airborne Division was to relieve us, while the Division went back to the TURNHOUT-TILBURG area for a little rest and much training. On the 25th January, the Battalion found itself in the little Belgian village of MERXPLAS, and its environs, and though by no means the acme of comfort, it did at least afford good shelter and opportunity for rest. Though even here we were not free from noise ; we seemed to be on the direct V.1 route for Antwerp and day and night the peaceful skies were rended by the spluttering sound of Germany's " war winner ! " A couple of quiet days were spent at the beginning in sleep and personal rehabilitation, and then on with the more stern realities of training for the breaching of the SIEGFRIED LINE defences. We were preparing, we hoped, for our last and decisive battle in the West. But where and when it was to take place we did not know. Conferences and planning went on apace and by Friday 2nd February, Company Commanders had been briefed. On Sunday, 4th February, the Corps Commander, General Horrocks, addressed all officers in the Division and revealed the whole vast operation. It was to be bigger than anything we had ever attempted before, and once again it was our Division that had been allotted the most difficult and vital part of the operation—the capture of CLEVE and the opening of the roads to the River RHINE and its bridges. Our task, too, as a Battalion was no easy one for though we were to avoid the actual breaching of the SIEGFRIED LINE, we were to advance with our left flank completely open for twenty-four hours. All the rest of Sunday and Monday there were conferences, and late on Monday evening we moved off to our concentration area at NIJMEGEN. The roads were full of other traffic and badly cut up by the sudden thaw and the immense amount of transport that had already passed by. It was a long, wearisome journey and it was after 4 a.m. on Tuesday, 6th February, before the bulk of the Battalion reached its billets. All Tuesday and Wednesday were spent in conferences, recces, briefing and preparations for the test ahead. By Wednesday evening, 7th February, all was ready, and we awaited the dawn move to the Forming up Point (F.U.P.) and the opening of the offensive at 10.30 hours on Thursday, 8th February.

Just prior to leaving MERXPLAS, we underwent a complete change of command and found ourselves saying a rather sudden farewell to Lt.-Col. Mackley and Major Wood, the 2 i/c. We welcomed in their place Lt.-Col. R. A. Bramwell Davis and Major F. B. B. Noble, O.B.E., both Regular Officers of the Regiment.

KRANENBURG AND THE SIEGFRIED LINE

We were astir early on Thursday morning ; breakfast was consumed with apparent calm and, in the last quiet minutes of the morning, final preparations were made and conferences held. At 5 a.m., the still hush was rent by the roar of 1,000 guns pounding away at German gun positions and, to its savage accompaniment, we gradually moved out of NIJMEGEN through the deep mud that once had been a country lane, to our assembly area. Here we met our tanks and marshalled ourselves in echelon for the advance. H. hour was not until 10.30 hours and there was a long, cold wait in the Forward Assembly Area (F.A.A.) before we could move to the start line and follow the Argylls through the gap they had made in the first minefield.

The original battalion plan had been to follow the Argylls through their minefield and then pivot left with three companies up—" B " right, " A " in the centre and " C " left. " C " Company were to advance along the NIJMEGEN-CLEVE road, force an entry into KRANENBURG and secure the western half of the village while " A " Company pushed slightly further forward and took the eastern half from the right flank. Finally " B " Company had to clear the railway station, hand it over to " D " Company and then execute a right hook and come on to the road from the right, rear of the town. To help us achieve our objective, we had an intense barrage 500 yards deep and lifting 300 yards every 12 minutes, medium bombers on Kranenburg, and the right flank squadron of the 3rd Tank Scots Guards, with various attached " funnies."

Owing to low cloud, the bomber effort was abandoned, and because of the deep mud and treacherous going between the start line and the village, many of our tanks and other supporting arms never caught up with the infantry, or only after they had completed their allotted tasks.

At 10.30 hours, 8th February, the Argylls crossed the start line and we began to move behind them. Soon all the " Flails " became bogged and the advance was slowed down as mines had to be cleared by hand. Almost immediately, " A " Company ran into an anti-personnel belt and lost several men, and eight stretcher-bearers were wounded before they could be extricated from the mined area. Once clear of the minefield, the Battalion swung left and despite the appalling ground conditions managed to regain and retain their positions close behind the barrage. It was a notable achievement.

By early afternoon, " A " and " C " Companies had reached the anti-tank ditch that ran north-south along the western approaches of the village. During their advance so far, " C " Company had successfully cleared RICHTERS GUT, a roadside farm, and another group of houses in front of the ditch. Meanwhile " B " Company, with the Carrier Platoon attached in infantry role, had been working up the railway and had reached a point just short of the station.

The first part of the attack had gone quickly and Companies consolidated near the line of the ditch, waiting for the barrage to lift beyond the village, and enable them to get in among the houses to clear and destroy the enemy therein. When the barrage did lift, " C " Company on the left went straight for the bridge that carried the main road over the anti-tank ditch. No. 13 platoon and Company H.Q. almost immediately came under heavy fire from a group of houses in front of the ditch. These were quickly cleared but, while positioning the piat, C.S.M. Donnelly was severely wounded in the head. Meanwhile, 15 platoon had reported that the bridge was intact and they pushed over it unopposed and consolidated the other side. No. 14 platoon followed over the bridge and 13, who with the opportune arrival of Lieutenant Scott-Barrett's Churchill troop, were able to clear the houses at top speed, re-organised and followed the rest of the Company over the bridge and into the village. Once the entire company was across, house clearing started with 13 platoon right, 14 centre, and 15 left, with one solitary tank in support, the other two being bogged on the outskirts. After some time, the main street as far as the lateral road was cleared and " C " Company task had been completed. For his great part in this action, Major I. H. Murray was awarded the Military Cross.

Meanwhile, in the centre " A " Company was having a more difficult time. The Company plan was for 7 platoon to secure the south-west corner of the village as a firm base ; 8 and 9 platoons would then start the house-clearing when the guns lifted. No. 7 platoon moved over very exposed ground to the anti-tank ditch but could not get across it as it was flooded and was covered by accurate M.G. fire. It was here that Cpl. Clapton sacrificed himself giving covering fire to enable his section to reach cover. Most of his platoon were either killed or wounded. Seeing that a frontal attack would prove too costly and too slow, Major Merrifield, M.C., decided to go round the right with his two remaining platoons and attack from the station area, which had been cleared by " B " Company platoons moving up on the right flank. This they were able to do in spite of heavy M.G. fire. No. 8 platoon were told to attack towards the centre of the village, while 9 platoon worked on the right. No. 8 platoon successfully worked their way along despite the unwelcome attentions of a Nebelwerfer that engaged a house they were clearing and which was ultimately eliminated by Sgt. Fletcher of " C " Company. About this time, Major Merrifield (commanding " A " Company) decided to follow 8 platoon and, though the gap between the station and the platoon locality had for some time been covered by accurate fire, he decided to take a chance. Most of his Company H.Q. got across safely, but Major Merrifield was killed as he crossed. The station now became a target for the Nebelwerfer, and for some considerable time was a most unhealthy place. Capt. Foulds, who had assumed command, decided to join 8 platoon by way of 7 platoon's old position in the ditch, and in doing so contacted " C " Company H.Q., where he learned that 8 platoon was doing excellently in house-clearing in conjunction with " C " Company. Having lost trace of 9 platoon, he came under command " C " Company until the end of the day. Later, 9 platoon rejoined, having been pinned down by accurate M.G. fire for some considerable time. Major Murray, " C " Company, took over the consolidation of KRANENBURG until some stray Canadians arrived to announce that they had captured it ! ! !

On the right, " B " Company had early on cleared the glass-house area of south-west of the village, advanced up the railway and secured the station. " D " Company had followed closely behind and took over the station area, while " B " Company pushed forward to clear a sparsely housed area east of the village. This, with the aid of the Carrier Platoon, they quickly achieved and by dark the task was completed and consolidation under way.

And so by early evening of Thursday, 8th February, KRANEN-BURG was ours—casualties had been fairly heavy, but the enemy had suffered much more, and into the bargain we had secured positions vital to the success of the Corps plan. That it was achieved with a bare minimum of close support, and under the most appalling conditions of mud and bog and in such a short time, is a remarkable feat of arms. No praise can be too high for the men of the Infantry Companies—it was a superb action.

Next day, 9th February, the Gordons and 44 (L.) Brigade passed through for the assault on the SIEGFRIED LINE defences. This was achieved with astonishing ease and in the late afternoon we were ordered to take over a position just south of NUTTERDEN, a village on the far side of the SIEGFRIED LINE. On our way, the road was accurately shelled by a heavy S.P. gun, and " B " Company had several casualties. By late evening we were installed and, by next morning it was quiet again, for our troublesome S.P. annoyed us no more.

At this time, news was rather scarce and very conflicting, nor was the position in CLEVE exactly clear. On Sunday, 11th February, we were ordered to clear an area of the town east of the canal, but after a day of waiting by the roadside in dismal rain, and just as dusk was descending, we were told that 44 Brigade had been held up in the western half and that we were to attack across their

OFFICERS — 14TH JANUARY, 1944 — OTLEY

Back Row—Lieuts. Seaton, Millican, Sharpe, Armer, Snell, Bowers, Nicholson, 2/Lieut. Blakely.

3rd Row—Major Hynek (Czech Army). Lieuts. Mitchell, Laing, Marr, Ewing, 2/Lieut. Weir, Lieut. Robinson, Odenhal (Czech Army).

2nd Row—Lieuts. Walker (R.A.M.C.). Agnew, Capts. Wylie, Struthers, Meechan, Lieut. Johnston, Capts. Campbell, Hay, Lieut. Bell and Rev. A. I. Dunlop, C.F.

1st Row—Capt. (Q.M.) Bain, Capt. Faulds, Major MacLachlan, Major Gourlay, T.D., Major Colwill (second in command), Lt.-Col. J. D. S. Young, D.S.O., M.C., Capt. MacPherson Rait (Adjutant), Major Johnson, Major Merrifield, Capts. Beatson-Hird and Scott.

SUPREME HEADQUARTERS
ALLIED EXPEDITIONARY FORCE

Soldiers, Sailors and Airmen of the Allied Expeditionary Force!

You are about to embark upon the Great Crusade, toward which we have striven these many months. The eyes of the world are upon you. The hopes and prayers of liberty-loving people everywhere march with you. In company with our brave Allies and brothers-in-arms on other Fronts, you will bring about the destruction of the German war machine, the elimination of Nazi tyranny over the oppressed peoples of Europe, and security for ourselves in a free world.

Your task will not be an easy one. Your enemy is well trained, well equipped and battle-hardened. He will fight savagely.

But this is the year 1944! Much has happened since the Nazi triumphs of 1940-41. The United Nations have inflicted upon the Germans great defeats, in open battle, man-to-man. Our air offensive has seriously reduced their strength in the air and their capacity to wage war on the ground. Our Home Fronts have given us an overwhelming superiority in weapons and munitions of war, and placed at our disposal great reserves of trained fighting men. The tide has turned! The free men of the world are marching together to Victory!

I have full confidence in your courage, devotion to duty and skill in battle. We will accept nothing less than full Victory!

Good Luck! And let us all beseech the blessing of Almighty God upon this great and noble undertaking.

Dwight D. Eisenhower

BRITISH TANKS PASSING THROUGH CAUMONT

MOVING FORWARD IN THE ADVANCE FROM CAUMONT   30TH JULY, 1944

MOVING UP TO TILBURG

NEAR KRANENBURG — 8TH FEBRUARY, 1945

THE RHINE, 10 A.M., 24TH MARCH, 1945

"D" COMPANY CROSSING A
BROKEN BRIDGE OVER THE
ALLER AT CELLE

CAPTURED PHOTOGRAPH OF THE
TYPE OF VEHICLE USED IN
COUNTER-ATTACK NEAR UELZEN

PRISONERS RUNNING IN
TO SURRENDER NEAR
UELZEN DURING "A"
COMPANY'S ATTACK IN
THE EARLIER HOURS
OF 14TH APRIL.

BETWEEN CELLE AND UELZEN — 13th APRIL

Men of a Rifle Company travelling on the Churchill tanks of the Right-flank Squadron of the 3rd Scots Guards. The Commander of 227 Infantry Brigade—Brigadier E. C. Colville. D.S.O., is sitting on the bonnet of the car in the foreground, together with Lt.-Col. C. Dunbar, D.S.O., Commander of 3rd Scots Guards.

LT. COL. NOBLE and LT./COL. BRAMWELL-DAVIS

THE PIPE BAND PLAYING AT AHRENSBURG JUST AFTER V-DAY

THE FAREWELL TO ARMOUR PARADE

SOME OF H.Q. COMPANY HAVING THEIR "TEA-MEAL"

21 ARMY   GROUP

PERSONAL MESSAGE
FROM THE C-IN-C

(To be read out to all Troops)

1. On this day of victory in Europe I feel I would like to speak to all who have served and fought with me during the last few years. What I have to say is very simple, and quite short.

2. I would ask you all to remember those of our comrades who fell in the struggle. They gave their lives that others might have freedom, and no man can do more than that. I believe that He would say to each one of them:

   "Well done, thou good and faithful servant."

3. And we who remain have seen the thing through to the end; we all have a feeling of great joy and thankfulness that we have been preserved to see this day.

   We must remember to give the praise and thankfulness where it is due:

   "This is the Lord's doing, and it is marvellous in our eyes."

4. In the early days of this war the British Empire stood alone against the combined might of the axis powers. And during those days we suffered some great disasters; but we stood firm: on the defensive, but striking blows where we could. Later we were joined by Russia and America; and from then onwards the end was in no doubt. Let us never forget what we owe to our Russian and American allies; this great allied team has achieved much in war; may it achieve even more in peace.

5. Without doubt, great problems lie ahead; the world will not recover quickly from the upheaval that has taken place; there is much work for each one of us.

   I would say that we must face up to that work with the same fortitude that we faced up to the worst days of this war. It may be that some difficult times lie ahead for our country, and for each one of us personally. If it happens thus, then our discipline will pull us through; but we must remember that the best discipline implies the subordination of self for the benefit of the community.

6. It has been a privilege and an honour to command this great British Empire team in western Europe. Few commanders can have had such loyal service as you have given me. I thank each one of you from the bottom of my heart.

7. And so let us embark on what lies ahead full of joy and optimism. We have won the German war. Let us now win the peace.

8. Good luck to you all, wherever you may be.

B. L. Montgomery

Field-Marshal,
C.-in-C.,
21 Army Group.

Germany.
May, 1945.

OFFICERS — JUNE, 1945 — LUBECK

Front Row (Left to Right)—Rev. A. I. Dunlop (C.F.), Major J. M. Foulds, Major D. A. Beatson-Hird, Captain R. C. Struthers, Lieut.-Col. R. A. Bramwell Davis, D.S.O. (commanding officer), Major F. B. B. Noble, O.B.E. (second in command), Major J. S. Hay, Major A. N. Scott, M.C., Lieut. (Q.M.) F. I. M'Gilp.

Middle Row—Lieut. S. S. Drew, Capt. R. S. Sunderland (R.A.M.C.), Capt. D. D. Farmer, M.C., Capt. W. Laing, Capt. A. R. B. Wylie, Capt. D. H. Struck, M.C., Capt. D. N. Steward, Capt. D. H. St. Croix, Capt. J. D. Robinson, Lieut. T. A. Dickenson, and Capt. D. R. Baylis.

Back Row—Lieut. C. C. Bintcliffe, M.C., Lieut. R. J. Jackson, Lieut. F. Hollands, Lieut. A. Wilson, Lieut. S. L. Hooker, Lieut. N. B. Hubbarb, Lieut. H. W. Simpson, Lieut. G. C. Hutchison, Lieut. T. C. Nolan, Lieut. A. Healey, Lieut. J. G. Coates, and Lieut. M. Timmons.

WARRANT OFFICERS AND SERGEANTS — JULY, 1945.

Front Row (Left to Right)—Sgt. F. Preedy, M.M., Sgt. W. Fletcher, M.M., C.Q.M.S. W. Forbes, C.S.M. T. Temple, C.S.M. J. Mullen, R.Q.M.S. R. Idle, R.S.M. M. Hooper, C.S.M. A. Paul, C.S.M. J. Wright, D.C.M., C.Q.M.S. J. M'Laughlan, C.Q.M.S. C. Smith, C.Q.M.S. J. Wood, Sgt. J. Woodman.

Second Row (Left to Right)—Sgt. W. Stansbury, L/Sgt. H. Scott, Sgt. T. Houlton, Sgt. J. Burrage, Sgt. A. Alden, M.M., L/Sgt. F. O'Neil, Sgt. I. Waters, Sgt. K. Hopkinson (A.C.C.), Sgt. H. Green, Sgt. W. Newton, L/Sgt. F. Patterson, Sgt. F. Shergold, Sgt. J. Robertson.

Third Row (Left to Right)—L/Sgt. R. Russell, Sgt. G. Pirie, Sgt. J. Parker, Sgt. R. Gardner, L/Sgt. S. Cooper, L/Sgt. J. Lang, Sgt. W. Smith, Sgt. J. Cullis, L/Sgt. L. Stuart, L/Sgt. L. Jones, Sgt. H. Clough, Sgt. D. Boardman.

Back Row (Left to Right)—Sgt. A. Hardie, L/Sgt. R. Snowdon, Sgt. J. Brown, Sgt. E. O'Brien, Sgt. G. Johnston, L/Sgt. R. Douglas, Sgt. D. Honor (R.E.M.E.), Sgt. G. Noel, Sgt. R. Paynter, Sgt. C. Smith, M.M.

"10th H.L.I. Crossing the Rhine"

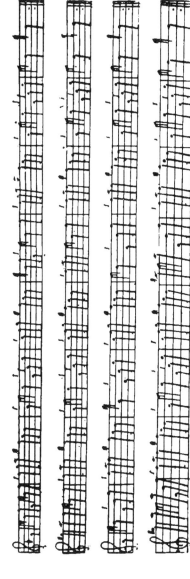

Composed by Pipe-Major Donald Shaw Ramsay and Corpl. J. Moore, 10th H.L.I.

front from the north-west, during the night. It was no small undertaking but, without further ado and with the minimum of preparation, " A," " B " and " D " Companies moved into the attack supported by the Scots Guards and some flame-throwers. In a surprisingly short time and with little or no confusion, the area was cleared and CLEVE had been rid of the last of the enemy. On Monday, 12th February, a Canadian brigade took over the defence of the town and the Battalion concentrated in the few remaining houses to re-organise. Though during the next two days the town was shelled and the odd bomb was dropped by jet-propelled enemy aircraft, it was a period of comparative calm and the rest was appreciated by all.

On Thursday, 15th February, the Battalion was originally scheduled to carry out an attack, mounted in Kangaroos and supported by the tanks of the Scots Guards, with the object of securing the high ground overlooking CALCAR and protecting the right flank of 46 (H.) Infantry Brigade who were advancing through the woods in that area. This latter task proved much more difficult than was anticipated owing to a gradual stiffening of enemy resistance. It was decided to place the Battalion under 46 (H.) Brigade and to limit our objective considerably. Moreover, the attack was to be postponed and done at night. We were to secure the high ground about 5,000 yards south of MOYLAND in a midnight attack, on foot, and then clear the woods on our left flank at first light on Friday morning. We were to have been supported by a squadron of Coldstream Guards tanks, but owing to fairly thick mist, the tanks were withdrawn at the last moment and our attack went in with artillery support alone. " D " Company were on the left, " B " Company right, with " C " and " A " Companies in reserve. " D " Company reached their objective, a ridge with scattered houses on the top and overlooked by the woods on the left, without opposition and started to dig in. An hour later, an enemy patrol appeared from the woods but was dispersed by Bren fire. Shortly afterwards, the enemy was reported forming up for a counter-attack and tracked vehicles were heard moving about, forward of " B " and " D " Companies. All our Anti-Tank guns and self-propelled guns had been bogged en route, and piat's were posted to guard the flanks. A self-propelled gun opened up on " D " Company from about 200 yards and M.G. fire swept their front. About 50 enemy then made a frontal attack on the Company, but accurate and intense L.M.G. and 2-in. mortar fire dispersed the enemy and they withdrew in confusion. Three of the enemy managed to penetrate the position but were quickly killed. All was quiet for a while until a similar attack developed on " B " Company, 500 yards to the right of " D " Company. The Company was still clearing a row of houses which included searching cellars and evicting both civilians and collecting prisoners of war who were mixed up together. With the help of two self-propelled guns and with our troops dispersed, as well as silhouetted by several burning houses, " B " Company's covering party was quickly overrun. There followed some close and confused fighting, and the superior weight of the enemy numbers drove the company from its position. The remnants, which included some who had been captured and then escaped, eventually went into " A " Company's position to consolidate. No further attack was put in by the Battalion as the ground lost was not vital, although it placed " D " Company—in front—in a very exposed position.

During the Battalion night attack, some 80 prisoners were captured, and it is almost certain that at least an equal number were killed or wounded. Fairly soon after the attack had been completed, the whole Battalion area was subjected to heavy artillery and mortar fire. It was during this period that our Padre—Ian Dunlop—was wounded by a shell close to the Battalion Command Post. He had been with us since D-day in Normandy and throughout every action had been indefatigable in helping to maintain the very high morale of the Battalion. Luckily his wound was in no way serious and his absence was not for very long.

At 07.30 hours, " C " Company started their task of clearing the wood but were immediately met with intense M.G. fire that precluded the possibility of their gaining even the line of the road that ran between then and the wood. After they had suffered several casualties, they were ordered to withdraw to their overnight positions.

Meanwhile, about 08.00 hours, the enemy under cover of mist formed up for another attack on " D " Company who were by now in a very exposed position with the enemy on their right and left and a 500 yards gap between them and the rear Companies. The concentration, however, was observed in time, and intense fire from artillery and the Battalion mortars forced them to disperse in disorder. No further attempts were made to attack the forward positions. The original intention had been for a Canadian unit to go through us and another and clear the woods. We were then to be relieved and return to CLEVE. The first part of the plan went well, but the wood clearing proved a very hard nut and it was not until three days later that it had been sufficiently cleared for us to be relieved by the Canadian Black Watch and retrace our steps to CLEVE for a well-earned forty-eight hours rest.

During these days, the area was subjected to heavy and accurate artillery and mortar fire—" C " and " D " Companies were the main targets, but Battalion H.Q. received its fair share of direct hits. No praise can be too high for " D " Company, under Major Hay, who for four days held on tenaciously to a precarious position with even more doubtful supply lines behind them. It was a great action and rounded off twelve days of fighting that gained the Battalion great renown and the personal commendations of the Army Commander, Corps Commander and Divisional Commander for its superb spirit and work.

After forty-eight hours, the Battalion moved to the BUCH-HOLT area, just east of GOCH, where it rejoined 227 (H.) Brigade. The Battalion relieved the 2nd Battalion The Glasgow Highlanders, and remained static for three days in a somewhat exposed position in the line, with " A " and " C " Companies holding the forward part and the other two Companies in reserve. " B " Company had one most successful patrol beyond our forward positions to some farm houses which " C " Company had reconnoitred the previous night and found occupied in some strength by the enemy. The patrol captured twelve prisoners without suffering any casualties. During this period, the whole Battalion was again subjected to heavy enemy artillery and mortar fire.

On the night of 24th/25th February, the Battalion was relieved by 1st K.O.S.B., of 3rd (Brigade) Division. The following day the Battalion, together with the remainder of the Brigade, moved to TILBURG for a period of rest, after having been almost continuously in action for seventeen days.

The following congratulatory messages were received :—

From Brigadier R. M. Villiers, D.S.O., Commander 46 (H.) Infantry Brigade on 19th February, 1945.

" When you were put temporarily under command 46 (H.) Infantry Brigade on 15th February, your task of carrying out a night attack was not easy. Late changes in the plan, and the fog which prevented at the last minute the use of tanks to support your attack, made your task all the more difficult. It was, however, vitally important that you should protect the southern exits of the forest and link up on your right with 43 Infantry Division.

In spite of the difficulties, you did the job magnificently. The confusion on the objective, which is inevitable after a night attack, was overcome quickly and efficiently. Then followed three days of remaining in your exposed positions, subjected constantly to hostile artillery and mortar fire.

I am very sorry for all your casualties you have suffered, but I want to thank you, and all your officers, N.C.O.'s and Men for your great effort. You may well be proud of yourselves, for you. have proved that you can " take it " and give back with full measure You have enhanced the reputation of your Battalion and 227 (H.) Infantry Brigade, and I know that Brigadier Colville will be as proud of your achievements, as I have been, to have had such a fine Battalion under my command for a few days."

From 30 Corps Commander to 15 (S.) Infantry Division Commander.

" Requested convey to you General Crerar's (Commander of 1st Canadian Army), admiration of the manner in which your Division has carried out its important responsibilities during the last fortnight of your heavy fighting. The Division has more than maintained its very fine fighting record."

From Major-General C. M. Barber, C.B., D.S.O., 15 (S.) Infantry Division.

" The Divisional Commander is proud to add his personal congratulations to All Ranks of the Division on their magnificent achievements since 8th February. Everything they set out to do they have accomplished and, by their deeds, they have enhanced the already high traditions of 15 (Scottish) Infantry Division. No one could have a prouder command and I salute you all on your great deeds."

THE CROSSING OF THE RHINE AND THE BREAK-THROUGH INTO GREATER GERMANY

The Battalion remained at TILBURG for eight days, most of which time was spent in resting and refitting. All ranks were allotted a period of 48 hours' leave in BRUSSELS. On 1st March, the Divisional Commander — General Barber — inspected and addressed the Battalion, congratulating all ranks on their recent achievements. The inspection was followed by a march past. The whole parade was somewhat spoiled by driving rain.

Late on 4th March, the Battalion got sudden orders to move to a concentration area at OPGRIMBY, approximately half-way between MAESEYCK and MAASTRICHT, on the west bank of the River Maas. The Battalion remained there for two and a half weeks, undergoing an intensive training period, which was chiefly devoted to practising crossings of the River Maas in L.V.T.'s (Buffaloes), preparatory to crossing the River RHINE. There was, however, some recreation, including a very successful dance in the village hall.

The 15th (S.) Infantry Division, 51st (H.) Division and the 1st Commando Brigade were the formations carrying out the Second Army crossings. In our Division, two Brigades were assaulting— 44 Brigade on the right and 227 on the left—with 46 Brigade in a reserve role. In the case of 227 Brigade, we were the right forward assaulting Battalion and the 2nd Argylls were on our left with the Gordons in reserve. The two leading battalions were to cross in Buffaloes, while the Gordons would follow in due course in storm-boats, after a firm bridgehead had been secured. The L.V.T.'s were manned by the East Riding Yeomanry, of whom "C" Squadron was responsible for transporting the Battalion across the Rhine. It was with this unit our preliminary training on the River Maas had been carried out.

The Battalion moved up into its forward assembly area in the HOCHWALD forest, just west of MARIENBAUM, on 22nd March. The crossing was scheduled to take place on the night of 23rd/24th March. Reconnaissance of the crossing places—half way between the towns of REES and XANTEN—took place. This was facilitated by the 6th H.L.I. from the 52nd (L.) Division, which happened to be holding that sector of the west bank of the river. For the previous week, brilliant spring weather assisted the final training being carried out, and on the 23rd meteorological reports forecasted another good day for the 24th. The 23rd was spent under cover in the forest with rest, conferences and final preparations for the crossing. It was undoubtedly one of the greatest operations to be carried out in the long history of the Regiment, and all ranks were proud that the Battalion had been selected as one of the assaulting Units for this hazardous enterprise. In the evening amongst the trees and ferns of the Hochwald forest, and screened from the air by the foliage, the whole Battalion attended an impressive service conducted by our Padre, who had lately returned completely healed of his wound. There we prepared ourselves before God for the testing days ahead.

Soon after midnight on the night of 23rd/24th March, the Battalion embarked in 36 Buffaloes, some two miles away from the Rhine, and at about 00.30 hours the Battalion column slowly moved across country in line ahead, in the order of assaulting, namely "A" and "C" Companies first, then "B" and "D" Companies together with Battalion Headquarters, and then 12 Buffaloes, with some essential vehicles like 6-pounder guns and towers, medical jeeps and some carriers for the carriage of wireless sets. Each Infantry Company had six Buffaloes, and there were certain supporting units whom we were also carrying, such as a section of Vickers Machine Guns from the Middlesex Regiment, some representatives of the Bank Control Unit (5th Royal Berks), and a special detachment of the R.A.M.C., for the evacuation of casualties on the far bank. Specially shaded lights guided the course of the Buffaloes, and the whole thing looked like some enormous reptile creeping forward in the dark. The noise of the vehicles was drowned by the terrific noise of our guns which had been firing continuously in one long roar since 6 p.m. The criss-crossing of the Bofors tracer, the roar and the magnificent firework effect of the rocket unit's projectiles, the pepper-potting by massed medium machine guns and the booming of the heavy, medium and field artillery, gave added stimulus to our expectations of a successful crossing.

On reaching a quarter of a mile from the bank, and at a point where the leading vehicle reached the river dyke, the Buffaloes split up and fanned out into their assaulting waves with "C" Company on the right and "A" Company on the left. The rest of the column then drew up with its head at the dyke, as it would not move down to the river until the first two companies had disgorged on the far bank. At 2 a.m. punctually, the first Buffaloes entered the River Rhine—everybody tense and expectant for the opening fire by the enemy. However, it appeared that our barrage had so silenced the enemy that no guns or automatics of any sort opened up and our two leading Companies were landed complete and safe on the far bank. Unfortunately both Companies had been landed sadly wrong and out of their areas. The general plan had been for "C" Company, who were right-hand Company, to clear the strong point of WOLFSKATH and then advance inland along the river dyke to occupy the village of OVERKAMP. On the left, "A" Company was to move down and clear the other dyke which ran parallel and about 50 yards inland from the Rhine itself. Then, after clearing down to the sluice gate which was our boundary with the Argylls, they were to move forward and occupy the village of REE. Owing to the wrong area of landing, " A " Company, instead of " C " Company, had to take on the clearing of WOLFSKATH, which turned out to be a veritable hornet's nest. Some confused fighting in the dark took place, during which time both Company Commanders were wounded. It was eventually cleared, but by this time the whole of the river dyke had come to life. It was eventually found that the Battalion front had a German paratroop battalion with most of its strength forward on the reverse side of the river dyke. " A " Company had lost all its officers, and began moving up the " C " Company axis, by accident in the dark, thus leaving the river dyke itself uncleared. They were closely followed by " C " Company. For his initiative in taking command of " A " Company, and his bravery afterwards, C.S.M. John Wright was awarded the D.C.M.

In the meantime, " B " and " D " Companies and Battalion H.Q. had entered the Rhine, and crossed without being engaged, except by the " Overs " from the fighting described above. They, like the leading wave, were also landed wrongly. Unfortunately, as the river dyke looked the same everywhere, the mistake was not realised by all concerned, particularly Battalion H.Q., who thought they were in fact in the right place to the left of WOLFS-KATH. Eventually " B " Company moved past Wolfskath and started to clear the river dyke, while " D " Company remained at Wolfskath as a fire base. It had originally been planned for " D " Company to push on up the centre and capture the village

" A " and " C " Companies advanced inland about 400 yards, but were held up for a considerable time by a 20-mm. gun which was raking the whole Battalion bridgehead area. This was eventually eliminated single-handed by Lieut. Picken, who tragically lost his life in so doing. About dawn, " D " Company advanced from WOLFSKATH and went through " A " and " C " Companies and eventually occupied the village of OVERKAMP. They were just too late to catch a German H.Q., as it hurriedly departed by car.

It was about this time that an interesting incident occurred to two of the Battalion Stretcher Bearers—L/Cpl. J. Donovan and Pte. W. Begbie. These two were accompanying " D " Company. A German stretcher bearer came forward from one of the German posts and requested medical aid. Both Donovan and Begbie volunteered and went forward with the intention of persuading the enemy in front to surrender. This project bore no fruit, and they were next seen being taken away by a group of enemy. Fire was opened up on their captors, most of whom succeeded in getting away with their two prisoners. They were taken back to the enemy Command Post, a large farm some 1,000 yards in the rear. They were taken down into the cellar where the Parachute C.O. greeted them by saying, " English very good ! "—presumably the only words he knew ! And then, through an English-speaking officer, asked them to join forces with him, offering good pay, plenty of food and liberty to walk out at night ! The offer was declined. Meanwhile, casualties were coming in every few minutes—Begbie estimated turnover was between 30 and 40 during his stay—and our two men lent a hand. During this period one of the heaviest artillery concentrations was put down in the area—so heavy that the Germans thought they were being attacked from the air. After our men had been there a couple of hours, the enemy started to withdraw—a move for which they had long been prepared—but, before doing so, the C.O. arranged a safe conduct for our men back to our lines. He bade them goodbye, thanked them for their assistance, and went out into the courtyard where three cars awaited him and his staff. At that moment, artillery destroyed two of them, and the last seen of the party was eight officers piled into one small car heading eastwards. Begbie and Donovan then passed through the rearguard that had been left and tried to make them surrender, but without avail.

In the meanwhile, " B " Company, under the able leadership of Major D. A. Beatson-Hird, who had commanded the Company in all actions since D-day, was making slow but steady progress along the river dyke itself. They were exactly twelve spandau positions to be eliminated. These were systematically dealt with, and in many cases by the individual gallantry of officers and Other Ranks, Lieutenant Farmer and Sgt. Scanlon being afterwards awarded decorations for their part. Later, a link was made at the sluice gate with the Gordon Highlanders who had taken the place of the Argylls in clearing their part of the river dyke towards us. Battalion H.Q., together with the Carrier Platoon, soon after landing had advanced inland about three hundred yards over the river dyke in accordance with previous plans. At the time it was thought that " A " and " C " Companies were further ahead inland than they were really. As a result, the whole H.Q. got into a most exposed position and they were eventually engaged at close quarters by the enemy. At dawn, Battalion H.Q. retired back to the WOLFSKATH area where they remained established till the early afternoon. It was during this retirement that the complete Royal Artillery O.P. party was ambushed and killed. This included Major J. Oliver, M.C., who had been gunner-adviser to the Battalion throughout the whole campaign from Normandy onwards.

At about 09.00 hours on the 24th March, the Battalion assault echelon of transport was able to come over and the Royal Engineers were able to start bridging operations in our beach-head area. At 10.00 hours, the air armada of Dakotas and gliders carrying the 6th Airborne Division and the U.S. 82nd Airborne Division flew over the Battalion area and dropped their personnel about three miles inland. This heartening sight was not only a great relief to all concerned, but it was also a magnificent spectacle. It made doubly sure that the infantry bridgeheads could be easily consolidated and enlarged.

About mid-day, the Seaforths from 46 (H.) Brigade, together with some D.D. (swimming) tanks, advanced inland and captured the villages of MEHR and REE. The remainder of the Battalion later moved forward and joined the other Companies in the village of OVERKAMP. Here the Battalion remained in reserve for the next 24 hours.

At the end of the first day the Battalion could look over its shoulder with pride in its great achievement. Our furthest objectives had not been attained, but these had been planned for a weakly held sector. Instead, the Battalion met a complete Parachute Battalion of the 7th Paratroop Division who were fighting fanatically and to the last. It was the great fortitude of leaders and the general fighting tenacity of the whole Battalion that enabled the bridgehead to be successfully established. Under such circumstances, this achievement could not be without heavy cost and our total casualties were three Officers killed and four wounded, and fourteen Other Ranks killed and seventy wounded.

On the 25th March, during the night, the Battalion moved forward and took over a sector of the front held by the Seaforths and Cameronians, in front of the villages of MEHR and HAFFEN. On 26th March, our positions were pushed further forward and " C " Company occupied BILLINGHOVEN, a moated schloss, with the help of an artillery barrage. However, there was no opposition as the Germans had retired earlier in the day.

On the 28th, with the help of flame-throwers, and in conjunction with the Gordons on our left, SONSKELD WOOD was occupied. This had previously defied all attempts by 46 (H.) Infantry Brigade to clear it. As in the case of BILLINGHOVEN, the Germans had vacated during the night and no opposition was encountered. " B " Company had several casualties, due to mines, which were freely strewn in SONSKELD WOOD, and very stout work was done by the Pioneer Officer, Lieut. D. S. S. Marr, and the Pioneer Platoon, who also neutralised some bombs which were laid in the main road through the wood. For the next five days, the Battalion remained close to HALDERN, a village some three miles east of the Rhine. Two parties of reinforcements, consisting in all of four Officers and ninety Other Ranks, joined the Battalion.

During this time, the armoured formations of the Second Army were fanning out across Northern Germany and Holland, while further south, the Ruhr was cut off by the First and Ninth U.S. Armies.

THE FOLLOWING MESSAGE WAS RECEIVED FROM GENERAL BARBER.

" I am extremely proud to be able to pass on to all ranks the following messages received from Lt.-Gen. Sir Miles Dempsey, K.C.B., D.S.O., M.C., Commander Second Army, and from

Lt.-Gen. N. M. Ritchie, C.B., C.B.E., D.S.O., M.C., Commander 12 Corps, and I direct that these messages be read out to all ranks on parade :—

From Lt.-Gen. Sir Miles Dempsey, K.C.B., D.S.O., M.C., Commander Second Army.

" The Battle of the RHINE has now been won, and the breakout from the bridgehead is well under way.

Your Division was one of two, which carried out the assault crossing of the river.

You defeated the enemy on the other side, and made possible all that followed.

A great achievement.

I send you and the Division my very sincere congratulations.

I am sure you are all very proud of what you have done."

From Lt.-Gen. N. M. Ritchie, C.B., C.B.E., D.S.O., M.C., Commander 12 Corps.

" Now that you are out of the immediate battle, I feel that I must write and congratulate the Division on the great achievement of forcing the crossings over the RHINE.

No one pretends that this was an easy job ; it was a mighty difficult one. That the operation was so successful was due entirely to the fighting qualities of the Division. Personally I am tremendously proud to have been able to take part in this venture, but much more so that the operation was carried out by a formation from our own country. Will you pass on to all those under you how highly we all think of you in this Corps ? I am afraid that I have often asked you to carry out very hard jobs. You have never failed. The present operations, I hope, may well develop into a pretty liquid party, so that I hope before long you will be up in the forefront again.

It is a great memory to me to know that the two crossings over the SEINE and the RHINE have been carried out by your Division for the 12 Corps.

I send you my very best congratulations on a difficult task magnificently performed."

No praise could be higher than these, and I am indeed proud to have the honour of commanding such a fine Division. I thank one and all for their fine fighting qualities which have carried us through all the hard times we have had from the NORMANDY beaches to the RHINE.

(Signed) C. M. BARBER,
Major-General Commanding 15 (S.) *Inf. Div.*

THE START OF THE CHASE

We had been living on the edge of expectancy for a day or two when suddenly, in the morning of Tuesday, April 3rd, we received the order we had all been waiting for—the warning order to move forward. Since the time when the bridgehead had become a break-through, we had been sitting as it were in a backwater while sensational news came through of the advance of the armoured divisions. Now, when we received our final instructions, it was apparent that we should be taking a large step towards catching up with the battle again. Company Commanders went forward in recce. parties well beyond BOCHOLT, and the Commanding Officer went forward to meet the Brigadier.

At this time supply axes were still few, and by the time the parties had fought their way through the traffic to the R.V. at HEEK—48 miles on—it was discovered that order and counter-order had followed each other so rapidly that even the Divisional Commander was at a loss. Then, finally, the Corps Commander drove up to say that the Division had now come under command of 8 Corps in order to exploit the considerable success they had achieved in striking deeply eastward into the Reich with com-paratively small forces.

For the Battalion, the move forward next day to the concentration area at EMSDETTEN—on the River EMS, between MUNSTER and RHEINE—was a new experience. Here for the first time, we were travelling through a large stretch of Germany where battles had been fewer and where civilians still lived—as opposed to the battle-town, flooded and depopulated districts we had known west of the RHINE. In passing through BOCHOLT we were able to see, better than we had before, the effect of heavy bombing on a town of any size.

Apart from that, our chief new impression of Germany was of the immense number of non-Germans. In every town and village, on every road and by-way, were some of Germany's host of slave workers ; in twos and threes, in dozens, in scores ; on bicycles and handcarts, farm-carts and tractors, in broken-down cars and trailers, they headed west ; some wild with excitement, cheering and waving at us, others still a little bewildered, plodding soberly by on foot ; French, Poles, Yugoslavs, Italians, Dutchmen and Belgians—and Russians, Russians of every shape, size and feature, from the UKRAINE to the limits of MONGOLIA—generally carrying some kind of a flag of the country to which they belonged.

In EMSDETTEN, untouched by shells or bombs, this semblance of a liberation was increased by the holiday atmosphere that prevailed amongst the population. Shops were open and crowds walked about the streets, having nothing else to do. To us, with memories of desolation like CLEVE and GOCH, it was a new thing. But German friendliness was, in fact, less than it appeared, as we discovered a day later when we heard of a British soldier being stoned in this " friendly " town.

We were told now, on the 4th, that our task was to take over the advance, in conjunction with the tanks of the 6th Guards Tank Brigade, from the 11th Armoured Division and 6th Airborne Division who were now pushing on beyond OSNABRUCK to the River WESER, near the historic battlefield of MINDEN.

The next day, 5th April, was spent in the intermediate task of searching a wooded area between EMSDETTEN and OSNA-BRUCK. Since Corps H.Q. was already far ahead of this, there was a slight air of unreality about the operation, and nothing more exciting than a small dump of petrol was found. The Battalion's recce. parties had preceded it, and at the end of the day Companies were able to move straight in to their billets in the western suburbs of OSNABRUCK.

After a day's enforced rest while the country was scoured for the T.C.V.'s which were to take us forward, we set off again on the 7th to concentrate in an area a few miles behind the WESER, to the north of MINDEN. The armour had by now secured crossings over the river and the task of the 15th (Scottish) Infantry Division was to break through on the line CELLE-UELZEN to reach the River ELBE.

In passing through OSNABRUCK, we were able to see again at first hand the devastating effect of the work our heavy bombers had done on the German cities. Large areas of the town, especially near the railway yards, were completely laid waste and, in many cases, even the streets were obliterated. We began to realise the strategic difficulties of supply and movement that must have beset the Germans.

By the evening the majority of the Battalion was in its billets in the attractive small village of WARMSEN : but " B " and " C " Companies had to follow up next day when more troop-carrying transport became available. While plans were made and reconsidered, we were able to profit by a few quiet days to rest and organise ourselves for future battles. The Pipe Band, having caught us up again at last, inflicted the full penalty of defeat on the local population by playing Retreat in the village. The Padre was very pleased to be able to hold a service once more in a proper church and not in a barn or an orchard.

After two days here, orders came for us to be prepared to move again, this time to our final concentration area beyond the WESER. And so by the 10th April, exactly a week after moving forward from the RHINE, we had caught up with the battle again. We reached WUNSTORF, over the River WESER, and were even, at long last, in front of the elusive and ever-mobile Corps H.Q. What is more, we were side by side again with our old companions in many battles—the Scots Guards Tanks.

WUNSTORF was a pretty village in spite of the war having passed through it, but we did not have long to appreciate it, for a night " O " group and an early morning start—that most annoying of all features of a successful advance—set us off on the road for CELLE. At last the Division had taken over the lead again, and it was through as yet unsearched country that we advanced behind the Gordons on that morning of the 11th April. Our progress was unspectacular and slow, crossing the River LEINE at NEUS-TADT, and crawling forward, village by village, while the Gordons in front mopped up small bodies of enemy who still wished to offer resistance. For us behind them, it was a day of long halts on the road—a God-send to the " brewers-up " of tea—watching the steady trickle past us of another hundred or so liberated slave workers in the most variegated assortment of clothing imaginable.

In the evening, the Gordons were still battling on the fringe of Celle with oddments of battle schools, convalescent homes, railwaymen and officer-cadets. Having covered 32 miles, we sat parked meanwhile in the stifling atmosphere of the woods which had been set alight as the tanks advanced. Finally, as dusk fell, we pulled in for our evening meal and to prepare for our part in the battle for Celle that night. We knew better than to expect rest, for when we took over the advance, we were told that it would go on, if possible, for 24 hours a day.

The small hours of the morning, then, found us passing through the Gordons to attack Celle and cross the River ALLER, the last major river in our path before the ELBE. The Gordons ultimately had been held up only by the necessity for bridging a crater, and prisoners reported Celle to be full of hospitals but empty of troops. When " A " and " C " Companies went forward into the town, they were able to launch their assault boats and cross without trouble so that dawn found " A " " B " and " C " Companies holding a bridgehead on the far bank. Celle woke and rubbed its eyes to see " Jocks " prowling round the streets. Indeed, in the dark before dawn, it is said that a voice from a window asked one of our leading Companies with its tanks if they were the expected Panzer reinforcements. The answer was robustly negative ! ! ! Across the river that morning there was a general holiday atmosphere as the Companies, deprived by the river of their own transport, toured their bridgehead in the most opulent of Mercedes ! By probing out on the right flank, the Brigade had captured intact a bridge over the river and the rest of the day was spent in somewhat laboriously passing the transport in a long detour over the rickety wooden structure and through sandy woodland tracks to get it to a point 200 yards from where it started.

TO UELZEN

Apart from the usual orders late at night, we were able to get some sleep overnight, but the next morning, Friday the 13th, we led the Brigade column off on what was to be a memorable 24 hours advance. " D " Company, followed by " B " and " C," all rode on the tanks of our Scots Guards squadron, while " A " Company followed up with the transport. We had been told to push on with speed and were in a mood to do so now that we had taken over the lead, if it was only to keep pace with the rapid advance of the Americans from Hanover on our right. It was irksome then to find our time being frittered away making detours round craters in the road, doubly annoying when we found that the German demolition party was obviously travelling down the road only just ahead of us. Once indeed " D " Company deployed a platoon to catch the S.P. gun covering this party, but it managed to make off under cover of smoke. Once, too, the Recce. troop operating with us had one of the demolitions blown under its eyes.

By 15.00 hours, we had advanced 15 miles and crossed, by means of a tank bridge, our fourth crater. Small batches of prisoners were constantly being brought in whenever a halt or a detour was made, and an occasional outbreak of shooting at some point in the column by a determined rearguard would result in some more coming in. The country we were travelling through, large tracks of thick fir wood for the most part, lent itself admirably to delaying tactics and we were always relieved to get out of the many " Bazooka Alleys " or " Spandau Corners " into an open patch.

Finally, at 16.30 hours, we were held up by our largest demolition to date. The trouble it gave us was increased by shelling from two guns nearby, and by the fact that delayed action bombs had been planted round the edge of the crater. After one of these had exploded, unfortunately with casualties to the Sappers attached to us, it was decided that work could not be carried out on the crater and yet another detour was sought, with the double object of by-passing the crater and catching the enemy who were defending it. " D " Company was left to guard the main axis beyond the crater and the rest of the column plunged into the thick woods north of the road. By excellent navigation on the part of the tanks carrying us — or by guess and by God — we made landfall on a lateral road beyond the crater, down which, in spite of a blocked road, the leading tanks and infantry were able to clear from a village the enemy who had been troubling us. After that, we withdrew into a tight " laager " astride the lateral road in the middle of the woods and sat down, as dusk came, for food and a few hours' rest. Although the deepening gloom in the woods made our position seem a very lonely one, it was in reality the enemy that was surprised. He obviously did not expect to find us sitting in the middle of his territory, and we had the pleasure of netting a lorry driving home from its day's work of preparing demolitions, a startled motor cyclist and even a senior officer in his car about to make his get-away.

Once again we were told that the advance was to go on by night, this time with the bold idea of breaking right through across country to the final objective at UELZEN, by-passing any resistance or demolitions that there might be on the main road. We were then given until midnight to rest, feed, and replenish with petrol.

Shortly after midnight began one of the strangest and most spectacular advances of the many we had carried out during our campaign. We were faced with a 15 mile advance along ill-defined and narrow tracks, through woods and villages deep into enemy-held territory, not knowing what demolitions or defences might lie in our way. But the exasperation of the day's petty delays had put us in a good mood for " bouncing " the enemy by night. And so we lurched through the night, with " C " and " B " Companies riding on the tanks, faced with the dilemma of burning off their boots on the red-hot engine plates or of being swept off by branches if they did not hold on securely enough. The dark, narrow forest tracks gave one the impression that whole divisions might be lurking on either side. Little wonder that a finger was on every trigger and questions, if any, were to be asked afterwards.

As the tanks roared into the first sleepy village, they disturbed only a handful of bewildered Germans in a couple of vehicles. Then came another bunch of prisoners, then a few more vehicles to shoot up, and so on into the next village, and the next, until we saw that we had really managed to achieve a break-through.

The crucial moment came as we entered the village of HOLDEN-STEDT, three miles short of UELZEN, about an hour before first light. As the tanks rolled in, we saw that this was to be " no ordinary party." A panic of flares and Verey lights rose into the sky, and the burst of fire became more numerous. A motor-cycle fleeing in the opposite direction provided good target practice for every vehicle that it was lucky enough to get past. Meanwhile, the leading tanks were through the village and heading for UELZEN. At this moment, they ran into a column of enemy vehicles coming towards them. In the ensuing shooting-match, an enemy ammunition truck was set blazing and blocked the road, trapping one of our own tanks in its flames. The column had perforce to halt, while pandemonium broke out all around. As we discovered later, we had driven right into a large flak site and part of the outer defences of UELZEN, which the GERMAN COMMAND were making every effort to hold strongly, even to the extent of committing what reserve of Panzer and Panzer-Grenadier forces they had left. Both flak sites and defences were just being manned, and some of the troops we captured had just dug-in after cycling down from Denmark.

As it was plainly not possible for the Battalion now to enter UELZEN, Companies were ordered to hold limited objectives on the ground they occupied, while the immediate area was cleared. It was soon apparent that we should not have things all our own way, for the enemy began infiltration and counter-attacks in large scale from our right flank. The first of these, just after daylight, was supported by a S.P. four-barrelled 20m.m. A.A. gun which suddenly appeared on the flank of rear H.Q. and " S " Company. With this gun almost literally raking the ground with its fire, the German infantry who followed were able to take prisoner a number of " S " Company and then man three more 20m.m. equipments on our left flank. A number of our carriers and four troop-carrying lorries were soon blazing under this concentrated close range fire, while " B " Company and H.Q. were pinned down beside the road. It was thanks chiefly to the magnificent work of our attached troop of artillery firing over open sights in the middle of the enemy fire that this unpleasant attack was finally dispersed. " A " Company was then able to launch a very successful attack, supported by tanks, on a troublesome wood feature further forward on the left flank. While the Company was still advancing across the open ground towards its objective, prisoners came running in from all sides, until over 70 had been taken, bringing the total for the night's work to nearly 200.

The situation, however, was still very difficult. " C " Company had been unable to advance very far on its axis owing to the approach of an enemy counter-attack. " A " Company was on an isolated objective and " B " Company was in a tight perimeter protecting Battalion H.Q. in the unhealthy area of the road from the parties of enemy in the woods only a few hundred yards to the flank. Part of rear H.Q. and " S " Company was split from the Battalion and fighting by itself on the road behind us. " D " Company had not yet rejoined from its task of watching the main axis further back. The C.O., having left for an R.V. with the Brigade Commander, was fighting in the area of rear H.Q. at the head of an improvised section of batmen and drivers. Reports of enemy infiltrating through the close woods on our right continued to come in, and the ground was still swept from time to time by one remaining 20mm. half-track. Also, " A " Company on their objective were being subjected to heavy mortar and enfilade M.G. fire.

The situation was finally relieved at 09.30 hours when a further squadron of tanks was sent to protect our rear, while the Argylls moved up to clear the woods on our right. The 20mm. guns whose close quarter fire had caused us such damage were eliminated, and we had the satisfaction of having one or two men escape from the hands of the Germans to rejoin us. " D " Company arrived and were sent to strengthen the left flank beside " A " Company. Intermittent shelling continued, but the battalion was now firmly in position with the Argylls on its flank.

During the rest of the day, the Battalion reorganised itself (" S " Company in particular, now had only one officer left), and prepared to continue the attack by night. The Battalion objective was limited to VEERSSEN—a southern suburb of UELZEN—while the rest of the Brigade was to pass through into the town if possible. Although the enemy had certainly been surprised by our sudden night advances—the evidence was in the prisoners and equipment we found—it was also apparent that he intended to hold UELZEN in strength, with a number of tanks and S.P. guns to support him.

A certain amount of rest was possible in the afternoon and evening, and half an hour after midnight of the 14th/15th, the advance into VEERSSEN began with " B " and " D " Companies leading. There was determined opposition in the village and some hours of difficult in-fighting developed. The severest fighting probably occurred when " D " Company was counter-attacked and shot up at close quarters by a S.P. gun : a number of prisoners seized the opportunity to re-arm themselves and join in the fight. The Company was split into groups which could not be re-organised until some hours later. The Company Commander only managed to escape by crawling away through a back garden.

When Battalion H.Q. entered the village just before first light on the 15th, fighting was still going on from house to house, the tanks being dangerously menaced by " bazookas " from every corner, while well-sighted M.G.'s covered every lane of approach for the companies. " B " and " A " had to begin a bitter game of hide-and-seek, yard by yard, to clear their areas, and progress was slow. At least six S.P. guns, each surrounded by a hard-fighting squad of infantry with " bazookas " and machine-carbines, and numerous M.G.'s and riflemen hidden in houses formed the defence that we were trying to prise out of this village. Several plucky attempts were made to stalk the S.P. guns with PIAT's, taking a snap-shot from the door of a house on the other side of the road. The score was one probable, afterwards confirmed as put out of action. The tanks were quite unable to advance under these conditions, but the Scots Guards were not to be deprived of a battle and joined in the yard-by-yard struggle on foot with any weapon they could find.

In this closely-packed battle, where adjoining houses were occupied by friend and foe, where sniping and snap-shots from the enemy S.P. guns or " bazookas " allowed no one to relax, the rest of the morning passed. During this time, the C.O., carrying out a recce. of a S.P. gun from some 50 yards away, was injured by a bullet through the shoulder and had to be evacuated. The work he had done in keeping the attack going had been tremendous. From then until the end of the war in Europe, Major F. B. B. Noble, O.B.E., was commanding.

The situation stabilised a little in the afternoon and, though the war of nerves continued, the Battalion now held some kind of line and could be said to occupy a position, if not the whole of its objective. The rest of the Brigade attack had, by comparison, scarcely started, for the Gordons had been unable to advance far beyond their start line.

That evening, 46 Brigade took over from our Brigade preparatory to launching a full-scale attack on UELZEN early next day, while 44 Brigade by-passed the town to the east. The enemy was apparently as glad to leave VEERSSEN as we were, for he withdrew that night. The Battalion finally got back to a rest area in HOLDENSTEDT by dawn on the 16th and enjoyed the luxury of a whole day in bed—the first rest worth mentioning that we had had in the last four days : thus ended one of the most strenuous actions we had every fought.

For the next two days we marked-time while the rest of the Division cleared UELZEN and the flanking formations pushed on beyond it. Then we were ready in turn to carry the battle to the ELBE—and across it if possible. Early on the 19th, with the Argylls in the lead, we pushed through the still-burning ruins of UELZEN on a march of 18 miles, which was to take us more than half of the remaining distance to the ELBE. By ten o'clock this peaceful advance through pleasant sunlit country had been completed and we began to question the necessity for moving so early in the morning. We had the satisfaction, however, of being able to carry straight through to SCHARNEBECK, some eight miles short of the ELBE. No sooner were we in occupation, though, than we were warned that the Brigade would close up to positions almost on the ELBE that night, and there was considerable speculation as to whether we should be able to advance straight across the river, rumours of the 11th Armoured Division having seized a bridge, and of parties of Commandos having been seen on their way to do an assault crossing.

The river, however, remained uncrossed and our task consisted in marching forward through the night to occupy LUDERSHAUSEN, 2 miles from the river, where we remained to cover the building of a bridge over a small river which lay in our path. Patrols were sent forward to the bank of the ELBE the same night to see whether a quick crossing would be possible, but they found that the nearby village of ARTLENBURG and other points on the road were occupied by enemy. During the next day—the 20th— an attack was prepared on these positions, and just before midnight " D " and " B " Companies moved forward to the attack, under cover of a good weight of artillery. There was a brisk but brief engagement at the entrance to the village of ARTLENBURG, and then the policemen who were defending it began to come in by dozens until nearly 200 had been taken. A further exploitation by " A " Company cleared the nearby village of AVENDORF without trouble. And so at last we stood on the west bank of the ELBE only four weeks to the day after crossing the Rhine. The memory of the advances made in that month, with the added knowledge that they were advances made into the heart of the enemy's own country, remained printed in our minds more vividly than any part of our campaign since the desperate battles of our earlier days in Normandy.

OVER THE ELBE TO VICTORY

Now that the immediate rush was over, we sat back to organise ourselves for a week of river-watching. (The Maas had given us long experience in this). The enemy, after our attack on ARTLEN-BURG, was singularly quiet, and except for the vigilance demanded of the outposts, life was fairly tranquil. " A " and " B " Companies remained on the river for the first few days, to be relieved then by " C " and " D ". At times the weather was so fine and the river scene so pleasant that the war seemed a very " phoney " one, and the Elbe might quite well have been some quiet river at home. It added to the peace and quiet, probably, that all civilians were evacuated from our bank of the river as soon as we reached it.

The chief work during these days fell on the O.P.'s on the river bank, manned by the forward companies and by the Intelligence Section. There every detail of movement on the enemy bank was carefully noted down until a very good idea was obtained not only of the enemy's positions, but also of his daily habits. " Ah, the mail has just arrived," the watchers would say as the sentry settled back in the sun beside his slit trench to read a newspaper. While the enemy was left undisturbed, he certainly led an amazingly casual life for a front-line soldier, coming down regularly to wash himself or his mess-tins in the river. Indeed we envied him the comforts he enjoyed, as we saw females flitting to and from his slit-trenches with food—or just flitting . . . On our side, too, life in the " safe rear areas " was quite pleasant for those who had the leisure to enjoy a little boating or fishing in the small river near Battalion H.Q.

At last, however—and with something of a rush, for they were brought forward 48 hours to the night of 28th/29th April—came the preparations for the crossing of the river by 44 Brigade. The two or three preceding nights were a great strain for the outposts on the river bank, for there were so many visitors " having a look " that it was impossible to tell friend from foe : a circumstance which, unfortunately, made it possible for three men to be taken prisoner by a German patrol. (They are now known to be safely released).

Whether it could have escaped the enemy's attention that we were building up our forces is very doubtful. Night after night along the cobbles of the single narrow road that ran down to the village on the river bank bumped a long stream of vehicles. By day every bush and building in Artlenburg, overlooked at the closest quarters by the oppostie bank, concealed one or more vehicles. In two days, from being an empty, uninhabited outpost, this village became the springboard for the last offensive of the war in Europe.

In the early morning of the 29th, the Battalion moved down to concentrate in Artlenburg. 44 Brigade had crossed at 02.00 hours and their bridgehead was already secure. Buffaloes and storm-boats were ferrying troops and supplies across, and at seven o'clock our turn came. Although it had not quite the Bank Holiday atmosphere of previous days, the river was still fairly peaceful, except for the blazing ferry house and a few stray shells ranging up and down the bank. It seemed, however, as though the Germans knew the H.L.I. were coming, for, no sooner had the storm-boats and Buffaloes started to ferry us across, than sizeable shells began to score direct hits on the steep and narrow lane which led up from the river to our new assembly area on top of the escarpment. There was no other way, so up we had to go at as much of a double as we could muster in the intervals of diving into the ditch. Our imaginations suffered more than our bodies, and we re-assembled at the top in good order, hoping that our transport would run the gauntlet as well. Although the Sappers on the river were now having a most unpleasant time, our stuff all got through sooner than we expected, and by 10.00 hours we were ready to start pushing out the western edge of the bridgehead.

Our immediate task was to advance some three miles through close and wooded country to occupy a rather empty " feature," while the Gordons on our left pushed down the main road through the forest to reach the river four miles west of our crossing place and then clear the pocket they had thus made. Opposition came from remnants of the Police who had been manning the bank, and from an indifferent collection of Labour Service youths who had been maintaining roads. " C " and " D " Companies, leading off through the wood, had to fight a number of small engagements, but prisoners came in at a good rate, and by the time " A " and " B " Companies had leap-frogged through " C " and " D " on to their final objectives, opposition had dwindled.

And so, in the afternoon, we found that we had crossed our last river—though we began to wonder whether, if the Germans proved stubborn enough, we should not be given the honour of crossing the Kiel Canal. Stubborn they certainly appeared at the moment, for the bridge site we had left behind us was receiving heavy shells at a steady rate, while the air was filled with more German aircraft—mostly fighter-bombers—than we remembered having seen in the whole of the campaign in Germany. A glance later at the cratered ruins in ARTLENBURG showed us that it had been a good thing to cross early.

The Argylls passed through us early in the evening to begin their night attack on the GRUNHOF factory area, two miles ahead ; while we settled down to a night of misery in a downpour with not a house to share among the whole Battalion. At 01.30, after food and an attempt at sleep, we moved up again to occupy two more " features "—an unconvincing name for a bald and exposed bit of ground—on the right flank of the Argylls. Our carriers lurched and whined along the mud tracks which we called our axis, calling down on us, as we thought, all the shells in the neighbourhood. However, the night made things appear more ominous than they were and dawn found all companies on their objectives without undue difficulty. Dawn also found the Battalion H.Q. and " D " Company in occupation of a large camp of Russian slave workers—a thing of which our maps had not warned us. As Battalion H.Q. had driven into the female part of the camp and occupied part of one of the huts, its position as the inhabitants came up in hordes into the daylight from their shelters was as embarrassing as any during this part of the campaign.

However we did not have to suffer the trials of this liberation for long. The cry was still " Push On ! " and the bridgehead was expanding from hour to hour. Resistance was crumbling all round, and in the afternoon we were sent to occupy the small village of Wiershop, a mile to the north, leaving " A " Company to form the tenuous link with the Argylls to our flank in Krummel. No sooner had we emptied sufficient houses for our use than the Gordons were on to the next village, two miles to the north-west, and we were ordered to move early next morning to Worth, another mile on in the same direction.

Thus, mile by mile, our front line began to ripple outwards in an ever-expanding circle from the point of our first crossing. Our Brigade sector was becoming extended to an extreme degree, but this gave little concern as the Argylls on the left were outside the town of GEESTHACHT awaiting its surrender. The excellent reason for wanting to surrender it appeared to be that it contained a stock of V2 fuel, enough to send both sides sky-high if it were accidently touched off. Further east, the lightning drive of the 11th Armoured Division and the 6th Airborne to LUBECK and WISMAR was massing itself.

Worth was occupied at an early hour on the 1st of May, the Recce. being already in possession. Companies took up defensive positions around the perimeter but saw little of the enemy. Before mid-day, a truce was in force on the Brigade front while the surrender of Geesthacht was concluded. We began to wonder if the war had relapsed into its " phoney " stage. However, at 17.00 hours, the surrender of Geesthacht had been completed and a reconnaissance of Hohenhern, the next village $1\frac{1}{2}$ miles to the north-west, showed that there were still enemy there who wished to fight. We were not allowed to deal with them until the next day, as our advance was to be co-ordinated with the advance of the whole Division on a three-brigade front to clear the Sachsenwald—largest obstacle still between us and HAMBURG, and reputed lair of Himmler.

At 08.00 hours on the 2nd, therefore, " B " and " C " Companies went forward to the attack, supported each by a troop of tanks from the Coldstream Guards. Some small arms fire on the outskirts of the village caused us to deploy, but with the fire support of the tanks we were soon enabled to deal with the enemy, and columns of smoke began to rise from the houses. (Even so, the tank men were heard to express disappointment that the village was " only half on fire "). About 40 marines were taken in the village— members of a Flak school in Hamburg. They said they had replaced some rather decrepit Wehrmacht troops the previous night.

They told us the truth, as we found when " A " and " D " took over the advance beyond the village through the southern fringe of the Sachsenwald. A little opposition appeared on the fringe of the wood, but when the tanks began to comb it with their Besas and the Companies swept through the trees on either side of the road, these decrepit Wehrmacht came streaming out and were made to run the gauntlet of the column, followed by loud objurgations from every vehicle. By two o'clock we were through the wood and tackling the next village—with the high-sounding name of Kroppelshagen-Fahrendorf. At the exit to this, " A " and " D " Companies and the tanks were held up for a while by two A.A. guns sited on the road. Some good shooting by the tanks and supporting artillery put paid to these, scoring a direct hit on one. " B " Company, meanwhile, moved along a parallel side road to give left flank protection. At 18.00 hours, it was apparent that we were still not to have things all our own way. An epidemic of sniping broke out from houses just short of the cross-roads in Neu-Bornsen—our final objective : the result was that all three leading Companies were temporarily pinned to the roads down which they were advancing, while determined bazooka teams held back the tanks. For a moment it looked as though night-fall would find us in a nasty position, after our previous successes of the day. It seemed to be the enemy's last fling, though, for the opposition thinned out and disappeared unexpectedly, just in time to enable us to concentrate in a tight perimeter defence around Neu-Bornsen cross-roads.

That night rumours were in the air, and the next morning— the 3rd—found us flying a white flag for the first time, for a truce had been imposed and the Commanding Officer was ordered to be ready from 17.00 hours onwards to meet the German Army Group Commander and conduct him to Divisional H.Q. for a surrender parley. We were disappointed, for the great man did not come ; instead, he sent a representative by another road to say that the commander was sorry, but surrender was already being discussed at a much higher level—in fact at Field-Marshal Montgomery's H.Q.

However, we were not altogether deprived of our amusement, for a spruce young German officer drove up in a large car with a number of men and explained ingeniously, with an American accent, that he was most surprised that he had been allowed by his own troops to drive through the lines into enemy hands, that he was only looking for the remains of his unit, and that, rather than trespass on our territory, he would return at once. He was told that, as most of his unit was already in the P.O.W. cage, he would be most cordially invited to rejoin it : alas, being a German, he did not appreciate the humour of the situation.

The news soon spread that Hamburg had surrendered, or soon was to do, and that our Corps had made a lightning dash to the Baltic, linking up with the Russians near Wismar. At mid-day, units of 53 Division took over from us and prepared to enter Hamburg : our Division, meanwhile, sidestepped northward seven or eight miles, the Battalion occupying the small village of Witzhave. We spent no time here, for we had orders to go on next day to take up billets in Ahrensburg. Peace was now very much in the air. Whole convoys of Germans arrived along the roads, driving themselves into captivity unguarded ; on foot, dozens of German soldiers trudged along the roads to give themselves up, or to attempt to reach their homes : they all told the same story— the war had ended ! As far as we were concerned, that still lacked official confirmation.

A pleasant day's march of ten or a dozen miles on foot brought us to Ahrensburg, where our harbour parties had everything comfortably "laid on" for us. Billets were good, and the place was a pleasant small country town, untouched by bombs or shells. Our eyes, trained by experience to seek the best accommodation, lit early on the Schloss, but it was found to be tenanted by a collection of deep-sea scientists and their paraphernalia—just one of life's little disappointments. Nevertheless, the whole Battalion was soon settled in very comfortable billets.

After our arrival, the proximity of Hamburg enabled the privileged few with transport at their command to take a trip down the Autobahn and view the city. There could scarcely be in all Germany a better monument to the terrible destructive powers of the Air Force. Those who went there, though they expected to see ruins, were overawed by the miles upon miles of complete devastation.

During the night of the 4th of May, rumours were becoming even more rife, and it was difficult to take the war seriously any longer. Finally, on the 5th, we were told on the wireless that our part in the fighting was over, and that the surrender had been concluded at 18.20 hours on the 4th of May.

Now that the news was at last confirmed, it was received with a strange mixture of feelings. The wild celebrations that many people had promised themselves mostly did not take place. It was difficult, on the whole, to realise that an end had finally been made to the campaign that had started last June on the beaches of Normandy. That the end was victorious, and that the victory had been won by some outstanding feat of arms, was probably not the main thought in our minds, as it would have been in the minds of the Germans had they been the victors. We chiefly remembered that the victory had been won by long periods of suffering and fear, by the loss of one after another of the circle of friends with whom the campaign had begun. It was in this frame of mind and with these memories that a large number of the Battalion attended a Brigade Thanksgiving Service next day, conducted by our Padre.

So, too, when the official VE-day was later announced, it came almost as an anti-climax. Fighting had already finished for us five days before, and we had got accustomed to the strange tranquillity and freedom from danger. The newspaper reports of VE-day celebrations, therefore seemed almost to refer to another war, such a time did it seem since " our " war had ended.

With the advent came, of course, blanco and drill. As one conference after another was held on the future employment of the army, we began to fear that the Peace would be worse than the War. It is true that amusements and entertainments were mentioned in discussions, but they seemed to figure rather small, among the ominous words check points, guards, ceremonial parades, drill competitions, inspections, barracks, discipline, etc. However, we had found some pleasure even in the middle of our battles, so we hoped to be able to do at least as much under the strain of peace-time soldiering.

After a good deal of haggling and bargaining for " occupation areas," we learnt that we were destined ultimately to live in Lubeck. For a week or so commanders at every level toured the countryside frantically to find themselves and their troops the most sumptuous houses available. Meanwhile, we had become so comfortable at Ahrensburg that we had to leave in order to enable Divisional H.Q. to heave its amorphous mass to rest in the town. We took up temporary billets for a week in small villages to the south-west of Lubeck, Battalion H.Q. being in ZARPEN. Here we ruled a large tract of the countryside and were chiefly engaged in rounding up some 800 German P.O.W. at large in the area, and D.P.'s (displaced persons from all parts of Europe, for whose lives it now became our responsibility to provide).

LUBECK

Then finally on 19th May, 1945, the Battalion moved into LUBECK, on the River TRAVE, and quite near the BALTIC, an attractive town comparatively unscathed by bombing, which was to be our occupation area. There was a lot to be done—guarding of factories, ships and displaced persons' camps, and innumerable problems had to be dealt with concerning our new relationships with the German people. Fraternisation with " displaced persons " and with our late enemies was under ban, and was by stages permitted until it seemed quite normal.

General Barber came to inspect us on the King's Birthday ; General Dempsey of Second Army came to say " Goodbye " ; Field-Marshal Montgomery came to thank us. The blanco arrived and the " barrack square " took over from the " slit trench." R.S.M. M. Hooper, who had done so much to train us before " D " Day, returned to make his presence felt. The Battalion took part and did well in the Brigade Drill Competition. In a formal inspection and parade, we said " Goodbye " to our Anti-Tank guns and Carriers which had served us so well. We began the old Football League again, and there were Company and Battalion Sports. The Pipe Band came into its own again, and the Germans of Lubeck heard the strains—even if they could not understand the mysteries—of the " doodle-sack."

Lieut.-Colonel R. A. Bramwell Davis, D.S.O., left us after leading the Battalion so gallantly, and Lieut.-Colonel F. B. B. Noble, O.B.E., who had been Second-in-Command and commanded during the closing stages of the War while the C.O. was in hospital wounded, took the reins. Major D. A. Beatson-Hird became Second-in-Command, Major J. M. Foulds commanded " A " Company, Capt. D. D. Farmer, M.C., " B " Company, Major A. N. Scott, M.C., " C " Company, and Major J. S. Hay, M.C., " D " Company. The Adjutant was still Capt. R. C. Struthers, who had been right-hand man of each C.O. in turn from the days of training and preparations in England and through the whole campaign. By his calmness, efficiency and hard work, he had contributed very greatly to the smooth running of Administration and the well-being and happiness of all ranks. The M.T.O. was Capt. A. R. B. Wylie, the P.R.I. Capt. W. Laing, and both had rendered the Battalion eminent service through the long year.

But Officers and Men began to leave us, some for S.E.A.C., some for other duties in the occupied zone, some for home and new drafts arrived to become part of us. The task we had set out to do was almost completed, and we all looked into the future, and thought of new duties and a new kind of life at home.

CHURCH

A word or two about the Church. When we knew that in a few weeks we would be committed in Battle, the Battalion met together one Sunday morning in a quarry at WISTON PARK, near STEYNING, and in a lovely rustic setting made our prayers to God.

On the first Sunday in Normandy, at VAUX-sur-SEULLES, again we remembered the task upon which we were embarking and asked for God's help. And steadily through the months of Battle— in the orchards of NORMANDY, in an upper barn at NORREY, on an island in the River SEINE, in the station waiting-room at MOL, in the Baptist Church at EINDHOVEN, in a Cafe hall at ASTEN, in the middle of the HOCHWALD, in a field at HAL-DERN after the RHINE crossing, in the old Church at WARMSEN, at LUDERSHAUSEN near the River ELBE—we were recalled to the Eternal truths which sustain all men, and gave " praise where praise is due." And then at AHRENSBURG, when the day of Victory came, we joined with the other Units of the Brigade Group, and gave thanks for our safety, our achievements and the Victory won—while, across the lake, the pipes played the " Flowers o' the Forest," in lament for those who had given their lives in high sacrifice for a great cause.

KILLED IN ACTION AND DIED OF WOUNDS

OFFICERS

204458 W.S./Lieut. J. A. BELL   "S" Wounded CHEUX, 26th June, 1944. Died of Wounds.

92317 W.S./Capt. A. BAIN (Q.M.)   H.Q. Missing (Presumed Killed), 28th June, 1944.

Cdn/154 W.S./Lieut. D. G. HILBORN   "A" Killed MOUEN, 28th June, 1944,

Cdn/25 W.S./Lieut. A. R. HARDING   "D" Killed, MOUEN, 28th June, 1944

293212 W.S./Lieut. W. R. ARMER   "D" Killed, MOUEN, 28th June, 1944

132503 T./Major R. B. MACLACHLAN
       "D" Wounded, MOUEN, 28th June, 1944. Died of Wounds.

62861 T./Major G. T. PALMER   "C" Killed, BARON, 17th July, 1944
(Devons)

143405 T./Capt. K. J. INGRAM   "S" Killed, CAUMONT, 24th July, 1944

189538 T./Capt. J. C. MURDOCH   "D" Killed, ESTRY, 6th August, 1944

113653 T./Capt. E. B. MOORE   "C" Killed, ESTRY, 6th August, 1944

172380 T./Major M. E. MERRIFIELD, M.C.
       "A" Killed, KRANENBURG, 8th February, 1945

276868 W.S./Lieut. J. A. KERR   "B" Killed, THE RHINE, 24th March, 1945

285864 W.S./Lieut. D. McVEAN   "C" Killed, THE RHINE, 24th March, 1945

162941 W.S./Lieut. I. J. J. PICKEN   "A" Killed, THE RHINE, 24th March, 1945

129008 T./Capt. R. T. JOHNSTON   "S" Wounded, UELZEN, 14th April. Died of Wounds, 26th April, 1945

KILLED IN ACTION AND DIED OF WOUNDS

OTHER RANKS

FRANCE

3196632	Pte.	BROPHY, J.	" A "	Killed, CHEUX, 26th June, 1944.
14256600	Cpl.	BURGESS, J.	" S "	Killed, CHEUX, 27th June, 1944.
3311557	Pte.	FARRELL, B.	" A "	,,
3326472	Sgt.	GRATION, H.	" A "	,,
3312490	Sgt.	KANE, G.	" A "	,,
3326323	Cpl.	MORROW, J.	" A "	,,
3316557	Pte.	McCABE, W.	" A "	,,
14424826	Pte.	REYNOLDS, W.	" A "	,,
3310013	Pte.	WILLETT, S.	" A "	,,
14322680	Pte.	HUGHES, R.	" B "	,,
14668962	Pte.	McGEECHAN, D.	" B "	,,
14326599	Pte.	PARK, M.	" B "	,,
3315847	Pte.	SPEEDIE, J. P.	" B "	,,
3312951	Pte.	DUNN, W.	" B "	,,
3327740	Pte.	BYRNE, J.	" B "	,,
3326399	Pte.	FLOYD, D.	" B "	,,
6982442	L/cpl.	KING, G.	" B "	,,
3326404	Pte.	GARDNER, G.	" C "	,,
7044908	Pte.	LIGHT, G.	" C "	,,
3193568	Pte.	McCALLUM, W.	" C "	,,
3326308	L/Sgt.	McGOWAN, R.	" C "	,,
3196813	Pte.	PETRIE, G.	" C "	,,
3327251	Pte.	McEWAN, R.	" C "	,,
3059398	Pte.	COWE, W.	" D "	,,
1514289	Pte.	PRIMMER, H.	" D "	,,
3536903	Pte.	HEWITT, J.	" B "	,,
3058954	Pte.	BROOKER, R.	" B "	,,
7044289	Pte.	RYALL, G.	" D "	Wounded, CHEUX, 27th June, 1944. Died of Wounds.
1441651	Pte.	ORCHARD, W.	" C "	,,
7044053	Pte.	WELLS, A.	" A "	,,
14550525	L/cpl.	WEBSTER, E.	" D "	,,
3320765	Pte.	JOHNSTON, R.	H.Q.	,,
7021905	Pte.	WHITEHORN, J. F.	" B "	,,
14689662	Pte.	PAIRMAN, A.	" C "	,,
3326216	Pte.	CAIRNS, J.	" C "	Missing, presumed killed, CHEUX, 27th June, 1944.
3326262	Sgt.	PROCTOR, C.	" C "	,,
3317260	Sgt.	McAUSLAND, J.	H.Q.	Killed, CHEUX, 28th June, 1944
3323381	Pte.	McKUNE, J.	H.Q.	,,
3327231	Pte.	GRAY, J.	" A "	,,

3326414	Pte.	GRAHAM, A.	H.Q.	Killed, MOUEN, 28th June, 1944.
1446317	Pte.	O'REILLY, H.	H.Q.	,,
3317585	Pte.	WILLIAMSON, D.	H.Q.	,,
14667116	Pte.	CHALMERS, R. J.	" A "	,,
3317593	Pte.	FERGUSON, A.	" A "	,,
3059808	Pte.	HANLIN, J.	" A "	,,
3316256	Pte.	McGAIRY, T.	" A "	,,
3066825	L/cpl.	McCLOY, P.	" A "	,,
1554468	Pte.	MULHALL, J.	" A "	,,
869288	L/cpl.	NIXON, E.	" A "	,,
3319266	Cpl.	PURDON, A.	" A "	,,
14406820	Pte.	BARKER, J.	" C "	,,
7044019	Pte.	ILLIDGE, J.	" C "	,,
3319948	Pte.	HAILS, R.	" D "	,,
3315410	Pte.	QUINN, F.	" D "	,,
14409491	Pte.	SHEARER, K.	" D "	,,
3314571	Pte.	SHIELDS, J.	" D "	,,
14410451	Pte.	WALKER, J.	" D "	,,
3310545	CSM	GENT, F.	" C "	Wounded, MOUEN, 28th June, 1944. Died of Wounds.
3316125	Pte.	CHISHOLM, P.	" D "	,,
3322059	Pte.	MURRAY, N.	" D "	,,
14540761	Pte.	HENDERSON, A.	" S "	,,
3325404	L/cpl.	ETCHELLS, G.	" S "	Wounded, COLLEVILLE, 29th June, 1944. Died of Wounds.
7044233	Pte.	ALFORD, J.	H.Q.	Killed, MONDRAINVILLE, 30th June, 1944.
3192946	Pte.	DICKSON, A.	" B "	,,
3328012	Pte.	McKENZIE, T.	" B "	,,
3316277	Cpl.	LONGWILL, W.	" B "	Wounded, MONDRAINVILLE, 30th June, 1944. Died of Wounds.
14678384	Pte.	GIBB, T.	" D "	Wounded, VERSON, 15th July, 1944. Died of Wounds.
14646673	Pte.	RAYNER, W.	" A "	Killed, GOURNAY, 15th July, 1944.
3312656	Pte.	STEVENSON, W.	" C "	,,
14200125	Pte.	LAVENDER, S.	" A "	Wounded, GOURNAY, 15th July, 1944. Died of Wounds.
3320079	L/Sgt.	OLDALE, D., M.M.	" S "	,,
3311502	L/cpl.	IRVINE, T.	" B "	,,
14499617	Pte.	HUDDLE, K.	" B "	Killed, BARON, 16th July, 1944.
3319968	L/Sgt.	WILKINSON, A.	" D "	,,
3317844	Pte.	FIELD, E.	" S "	,,
3536889	Cpl.	BRADLEY, J.	" S "	,,
5385938	Pte.	GREEN, F.	" S "	Wounded, BARON, 15th July, 1944. Died of Wounds.

FRANCE—continued

3311525	Pte.	MAXWELL, S.	H.Q.	Wounded beyond CAUMONT, 30th July, 1944. Died of Wounds.
6460732	Pte.	VALLER, J.	" A "	,,
3781564	Pte.	HORROCKS, K.	" B "	,,
14412489	Pte.	HORNBY, J.	" B "	,,
14681002	Pte.	PEDDER, G.	" A "	Killed, HERVIEUX, 30th July, 1944.
3315830	L/cpl.	PATERSON, A.	" A "	,,
3317223	CSM	HUMBLE, J. F.	" A "	,,
3326286	Pte.	SUTHERLAND, J.	H.Q.	,,
3455320	L/cpl.	SCHOFIELD, A.	" B "	,,
3195891	Sgt.	SMITH, J.	" S "	Killed, AU CORNU, 5th August, 1944.
3328021	L/Sgt.	MAJOR, W.	" B "	Killed, ESTRY, 6th August, 1944.
7044058	L/cpl.	SHAW, T.	" B "	,,
3326687	Pte.	SULLIVAN, M.	" B "	,,
3315443	Pte.	HUNTER, A.	" B "	,,
3328016	Pte.	McLAUGHLIN, W.	" B "	,,
14499130	L/cpl.	SELLWOOD, K.	" C "	,,
5440928	Pte.	ANDERSON, W.	" C "	,,
14412325	Pte.	SHORT, D.	" D "	,,
2079416	Pte.	WARD, E.	" D "	,,
5391203	Cpl.	PLAISTOW, J.	" C "	,,
5377678	Sgt.	BLACKALL, A.	" B "	,,
3313957	Cpl.	TAGGART, J.	" D "	Wounded, ESTRY, 6th August, 1944. Died of Wounds.
14406400	Pte.	SNOWLING, K.	" B "	,,
5388442	Pte.	ARNOTT, H.	" S "	Killed, ESTRY, 7th August, 1944.
5388401	Pte.	DAVIES, A.	" S "	,,
7044079	Pte.	MANSFIELD, L.	" S "	,,
1804115	L/cpl.	WALKER, T.	" S "	,,
3310213	CSM	DIXON, F.	" D "	,,
3316192	Pte.	BENNETT, A.	" A "	,,
5385776	Pte.	HANKS, G.	" A "	,,
3326203	L/cpl.	BROWN, A.	" A "	,,
14414799	Pte.	KEEBLE, W.	" A "	Wounded, ESTRY, 7th August, 1944. Died of Wounds.
4865327	Pte.	SYKES, N.	" A "	,,
7044077	Pte.	CHINNOCK, F.	" A "	,,
3326322	Pte.	MORRISON, A.	" A "	,,
14504055	Pte.	HANNAH,	" B "	,,
956743	Pte.	BROWN, D.	" C "	,,
1154761	Pte.	HARNETT, S.	" S "	,,

FRANCE—continued

7044141	L/Sgt.	BAKER, N. B.	" S "	Killed, near ESTRY, 13th August, 1944.
14410355	Pte.	CARTER, J.	" A "	Killed, LE BOIS HALBOUT, 20th August, 1944.
3066344	Pte.	SCOTT, T.	H.Q.	,,
4078142	Pte.	WAINWRIGHT, L.	H.Q.	Killed, SEINE, 27th August, 1944.
3909562	Pte.	COLLINS, W.	" A "	,,
989034	Pte.	LONG, C. H.	" A "	Wounded, SEINE, 28th August, 1944. Died of Wounds.

BELGIUM

14644429	Pte.	MACDONALD, J.	" S "	Killed near ESCAUT CANAL, 17th September, 1944.
3311323	Sgt.	HASSELL, J.	" A "	Killed, GHEEL, 18th September, 1944.
3058826	Sgt.	DAVIDSON, W., M.M.	" A "	Wounded, GHEEL, 18th Sept., 1944. Died of Wounds.
3659085	Pte.	DAVENPORT, J.	" A "	Killed, GHEEL BRIDGEHEAD, 20th September, 1944.
3317945	Sgt.	BROWN, T.	" B "	,,
14671652	Pte.	NIXON, R.	" B "	,,
3315393	Pte.	FULLERTON, A.	" D "	,,
3326301	L/cpl.	McIVER, D.	" D "	,,
955504	Pte.	OXLEY, T.	" S "	,,
2825065	Pte.	ANDERSON, J. F.	" S "	,,
7022306	Pte.	McHUGH, J.	" B "	,,
2939424	Pte.	BECKETT, N. B.	" S "	Wounded, GHEEL BRIDGEHEAD, 20th Sept., 1944. Died of Wounds in enemy hands, 23rd September, 1944.
1521048	Pte.	AYRES, V.	" S "	Wounded, GHEEL BRIDGEHEAD, 20th Sept., 1944. Died of Wounds in enemy hands, 5th October, 1944.

HOLLAND

3593864	Pte.	BREAVINGTON, J.	" C "	Killed, BEST, 26th Sept., 1944.
3385664	Pte.	KENNEDY, T.	" C "	,,
3600015	Pte.	MARK, J.	" S "	Wounded, BEST, 29th Sept., 1944. Died of Wounds.
2392221	Pte.	JOYCE, M.	" B "	Killed, BEST, 30th Sept., 1944.
7044083	Cpl.	PHILLIPS, G.	" A "	Killed, BEST, 22nd October, 1944
14204539	Pte.	SKUDDER, E. J.	" A "	Killed, ASTEN, 30th October, 1944.

HOLLAND—*continued*

14714044	Pte.	ROBINSON, G.	" C "	Killed, ASTEN, 31st October, 1944.
3597122	Pte.	APPLETON, A.	" C "	,,
14658752	Pte.	WAITES, D.	" A "	Wounded, ASTEN, 4th Nov., 1944. Died of Wounds.
5379505	Pte.	UNDERWOOD, W.	" C "	Killed, MEIJEL, 16th Nov., 1944.
14242419	Pte.	BAKER, A.	" B "	Killed, MEIJEL, 18th Nov., 1944.
3319956	Cpl.	MULHOLLAND, B.	" B "	Killed, BAARLO, 9th Dec., 1944.
5676694	Pte.	SEARLE, J.	" D "	Killed, BAARLO, 12th Dec., 1944.
4914284	Sgt.	FISHER, F.	H.Q.	Killed, BAARLO, 13th January, 1945.

GERMANY

7044206	Cpl.	CLAPTON, A.	" A "	Killed, KRANENBURG, 8th Feb., 1945.
3311149	Pte.	MEIN, J.	" A "	,,
1628120	Pte.	MILLER, H.	" A "	,,
1538715	Pte.	MERCHANT, J.	" A "	,,
14741093	Pte.	OSBORNE, A.	" A "	,,
14678362	Pte.	EASTCROFT	" A "	,,
14760257	Pte.	DUCE, S.	" B "	,,
1628590	Cpl.	KEMP, E.	" B "	,,
3328018	Pte.	McLEAN, R.	" B "	,,
14643875	Pte.	SPILLMAN, R.	" C "	,,
14746050	Pte.	PAMBY, G.	" B "	Wounded, KRANENBURG, 8th February, 1945. Died of Wounds.
3538857	L/cpl.	BOWEN, H.	" S "	,,
3311465	Pte.	MURPHY, J.	H.Q.	,,
7044012	L/Sgt.	COX, H.	" B "	,,
14770594	Pte.	GREEN, J. E.	" B "	Killed, KRANENBURG, 9th Feb., 1945.
4104566	Pte.	TAYLOR, T. A.	" B "	,,
4915903	Sgt.	FOSTER, F.	" S "	,,
2760251	Pte.	ANDERSON, W.	" C "	Killed, MOYLAND WOOD, 16th February, 1945.
14713950	Pte.	BROUGHTON, H.	" C "	,,
3318006	Pte.	HOUSTON, J.	" C "	,,
13096893	Pte.	OVAL, F.	" C "	,,
14497805	Pte.	RICHER, H.	" C "	,,
4539327	Pte.	GRIFFITHS, J.	" D "	,,
7045367	Pte.	SAUL, W.	" D "	,,
5385870	L/cpl.	SMITH, A.	" D "	,,
14772282	Pte.	STEPHENS, W.	" D "	,,
14654702	Pte.	TODD, R.	" S "	,,
1579674	Pte.	GOMM, F.	" A "	,,
1799008	Pte.	GEMMELL, A.	" C "	,,

3597894	Cpl.	ADAMS, C.	" A "	Wounded, MOYLAND WOOD, 16th February, 1945. Died of Wounds.
3597965	Pte.	COLLINS, A.	" S "	,,
14767030	Pte.	BOTT, A.	" C "	Wounded, MOYLAND WOOD, 16th February, 1945. Died of Wounds in enemy hands.
3322012	Cpl.	BEGG, J.	" S "	,,
3322215	Pte.	McNICOL, J.	" S "	Missing, MOYLAND WOOD, 16th February, 1945. Died of Wounds in enemy hands.
14749983	Pte.	REYNOLDS, A.	" D "	Killed, MOYLAND WOOD, 17th February, 1945.
14733705	Pte.	BURGE, A.	" D "	,,
6298334	Pte.	BOOTH, F.	" C "	Killed, MOYLAND WOOD, 18th February, 1945.
14643802	L/Sgt.	EASTMAN, W. S.	" A "	Killed, THE RHINE, 24th March, 1945.
14791833	Pte.	PAGE, T.	" A "	,,
14790477	Pte.	FORSYTH, G.	" A "	,,
14790179	Pte.	CLIFFORD, A.	" A "	,,
11005812	Cpl.	MORTON, G.	" A "	,,
1829087	Pte.	WHYMAN, A.	" B "	,,
14555988	Pte.	STENTON, G.	" B "	,,
14612998	Pte.	THOMSON, J.	" B "	,,
14763384	Pte.	LOWE, E.	" B "	,,
1543058	Pte.	PETLEY, P.	" D "	,,
14554463	Pte.	BREEN, C.	H.Q.	,,
14418882	Pte.	STRINGFELLOW, J. R.	" A "	Wounded, THE RHINE, 24th March, 1945. Died of Wounds.
14785381	Pte.	PICKLES, S.	" C "	,,
4919883	Cpl.	BAINES, M. T.	" A "	,,
3328039	Pte.	SMITH, A.	" C "	Killed, MEHR, 26th March, 1945.
4450739	Pte.	ROLIN, A.	" B "	Killed, HALDERN, 28th March, 1945.
972313	Pte.	JOHNSTON, J.	" B "	Killed between CELLE and UELZEN, 13th April, 1945.
14768382	Pte.	STEVENS, A.	" B "	Wounded between CELLE and UELZEN, 13th April, 1945. Died of Wounds.
3606100	Pte.	PINK, T.	" S "	Killed, UELZEN, 14th April, 1945.
14711175	Pte.	PINK, S.	" S "	,,
14825045	Pte.	DONOHUE, L.	" A "	,,
1639064	Pte.	GILES, C. T.	" A "	,,
14358273	Pte.	BROWN, R.	" C "	,,
1656081	Pte.	TILSTONE, J.	" C "	,,
3059593	Pte.	AIREY	" A "	,,
3194159	Pte.	RAE, G.	" A "	,,

3327961	Pte.	Egglestone, J.	" D "	Killed, Uelzen, 15th April, 1945.
14338575	Pte.	Kelly, H.	" D "	,,
14814566	Pte.	Meikle, J.	" D "	,,
3600221	L/cpl.	Thornborough, J. R.	" A "	,,
14825031	Pte.	Clark, W.	" A "	,,
14825084	Pte.	McClelland, J.	" A "	,,
1549077	Pte.	Mantle, H.	" B "	,,
7047671	L/cpl.	Drissell, A.	" S "	,,
14985182	Pte.	Ford, G.	" A "	Killed, River Elbe, 29th April, 1945.
14246910	Pte.	Hardie, E.	" B "	Killed, Hohenhorn, 2nd May, 1945.
1761186	Pte.	Evans, J. R.	" A "	Killed, Kropelshagen - Fahrendorf, 2nd May, 1945.
14732261	Pte.	Sherwood, D.	" D "	,,
2937322	Pte.	Bain, D.	" B "	,,
14834201	Pte.	Reid, W.	" B "	Wounded, Neu Bornsen, 2nd May, 1945. Died of Wounds.
3457766	Pte.	Gorman, J.	" S "	Killed, Lubeck, 8th September, 1945.

AWARDS

138556	Capt.	SCOTT, A. N.	M.C.	CHEUX, 27th June, 1944.
3325761	Sgt.	CAMPBELL, R. A.	M.M.	
3320079	L/Sgt.	OLDALE, D.	M.M.	CHEUX. (Died of Wounds).
172380	Major	MERRIFIELD, M. E.	M.C.	HERVIEUX, 30th July, 1944. (Killed in action).
3058826	L/Sgt.	DAVIDSON, W.	M.M.	HERVIEUX. (Killed in action).
6460216	L/cpl.	SCOTT-TAYLOR, A.	M.M.	HERVIEUX.
39640	Lt.-Col.	RUSSELL MORGAN, D.	M.C.	ESTRY, 6th August, 1944
3323885	Sgt.	SMITH, C.	M.M.	,,
4039943	Sgt.	DALY, P., M.M.	D.C.M.	SEINE, 27th Aug., 1944.
5722364	Sgt.	PREEDY, F.	M.M.	ESCAUT CANAL, 20th September, 1944.
3311619	L/Sgt.	McDONALD, A.	M.M.	,,
7044188	L/cpl.	RIDDICK, W.	M.M.	,,
Cdn/515	Lieut.	STRUCK, D. H.	M.C.	DONDERDONCK, 30th September, 1944.
5187671	L/Sgt.	DAWSON, H.	M.M.	,,
33622	Lt.-Col.	BRAMWELL DAVIS, R. A.	D.S.O.	KRANENBURG, 8th Feb., 1945.
67193	Major	MURRAY, I. H.	M.C.	,,
5382795	Sgt.	FLETCHER, W.	M.M.	,,
14554551	Pte.	LYNCH, J.	M.M.	,,
336653	Lieut.	FARMER, D. D.	M.C.	THE RHINE, 24th March, 1945.
3317002	C.S.M.	WRIGHT, J.	D.C.M.	,,
3328034	L/Sgt.	SCANLON, T.	M.M.	,,
33622	Lt.-Col.	BRAMWELL DAVIS, R. A.	Bar to D.S.O.	UELZEN, 15th April, 1945.
176939	Major	HAY, J. S.	M.C.	UELZEN, 15th April, 1945.
308288	Lieut.	BINTCLIFFE, C. G.	M.C.	HOHENHORN, 2nd May, 1945.
7043959	Pte.	CHARLESWORTH, W.	M.M.	(Periodic).
1702538	Sgt.	ALDEN, A.	M.M.	,,
129004	Major	BEATSON-HIRD, D. A.	M.C.	,,
5339602	Sgt.	STANSBURY, W. J.	M.M.	,,
14297264	Sgt.	ANDREWS, R.	M.M.	,,
143409	Capt.	STRUTHERS, R. C.	CROIX DE GUERRE with Gilt Star.	
3306350	Cpl.	MARSH, J.	CROIX DE GUERRE with Bronze Star.	
156596	Capt.	STEWARD, D. N.	SILVER STAR (America).	

MENTION IN DESPATCHES

241311	Rev.	DUNLOP, A. I. (C.F.)
143409	Capt.	STRUTHERS, R. C.
333143	Lieut.	HEALEY, A.
14406640	Sgt.	VICKERS, H.
3314102	Cpl.	MARINI, C.
111318	Lt.-Col.	MACKENZIE, I., D.S.O.
3195206	Sgt.	CULLIS, J.
156596	Capt.	STEWARD, D. N.
92548	Capt.	WYLIE, A. R. B.
336016	Lt.Q.M.	McGILP, F. I.
5382795	Sgt.	FLETCHER, W.
129004	Major	BEATSON-HIRD, D. A.
291128	Capt.	SUNDERLAND, R. S. (R.A.M.C.).
5339602	Sgt.	STANSBURY, W.

COMMANDER-IN-CHIEF'S CERTIFICATES

3308480	Sgt.	CHAPMAN, W.
3326194	Sgt.	WILSON, A.
3314977	L/cpl.	McGRANE, T.
4745393	Pte.	CATTERALL, J.
3314972	C.S.M.	MULLEN, J.
3058986	Sgt.	GREEN, H.
102028	Lieut.	MARR, D. S. S.
4975180	Pte.	BRACKENBURG, P.
14554529	Pte.	HEPBURN, S.
7044075	Pte.	REES, R.
3322083	Cpl.	TRAYNOR, E.
3317003	L/Sgt.	YARDLEY, H.
3314970	Cpl.	KANE, D.
3319938	L/cpl.	BENNETT, M.
3327976	L/cpl.	BUCHAN, W.
3319957	Sgt.	NEWTON, W.
138555	Major	REDDICK, A. F.
5051731	Sgt.	KNIGHT, A.
7046780	Pte.	CART, S.
3326343	Pte.	KELLY, J.
3316118	Sgt.	HARDIE, A.

(This list is necessarily incomplete, as all awards were not announced in time for publication)

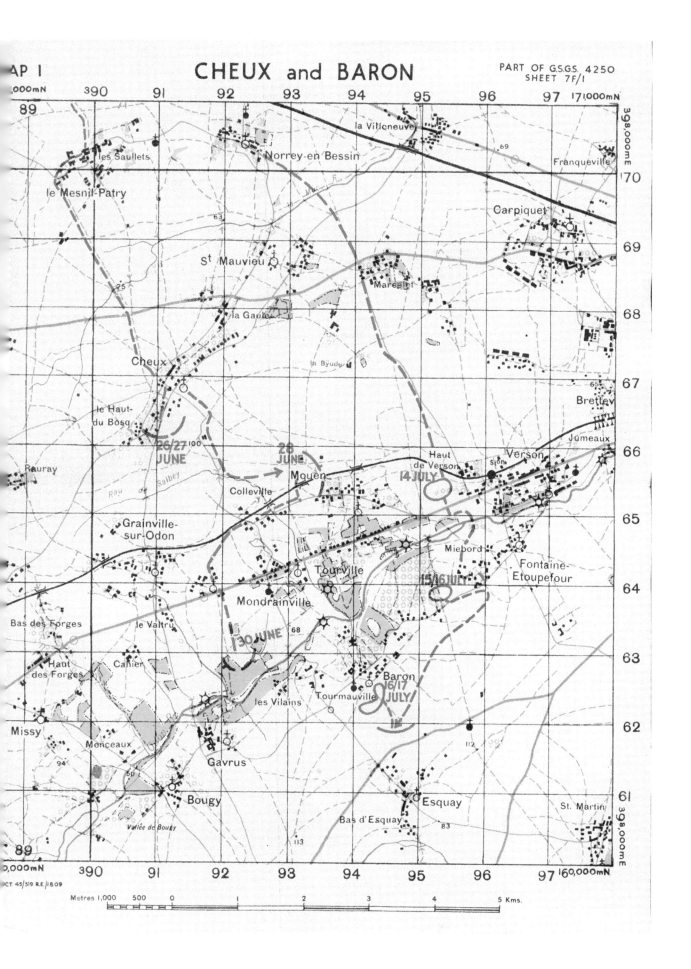

CHEUX and BARON

MAP I

PART OF G.S.G.S. 4250
SHEET 7F/1

390   91   92   93   94   95   96   97   171,000mN

398,000mE

les Saullets

Norrey-en Bessin

la Villeneuve

Franqueville

le Mesnil-Patry

Carpiquet

St Mauvieu

Marcelet

la Gaule

Cheux

la Bijude

le Haut-
du Bosq

Brettev

Jumeaux

26/27
JUNE   100

28
JUNE

Haut
de Verson

Sion

Verson

14 JULY

Rauray

Mouen

Colleville

Grainville-
sur-Odon

Tourville

Miebord

Fontaine-
Etoupefour

Bas des Forges

Mondrainville

le Valtru

15/16 JULY

30 JUNE   68

Haut
des Forges

Cahier

les Vilains

Baron

Tourmauville

16/17
JULY

Missy

Monceaux

Gavrus

Esquay

St Martin

Bougy

Bas d'Esquay

Vallée de Bougy

89

390   91   92   93   94   95   96   97   160,000mN

398,000mE

Metres 1,000   500   0   1   2   3   4   5 Kms.

MAP 2

CAUMONT TO ESTRY

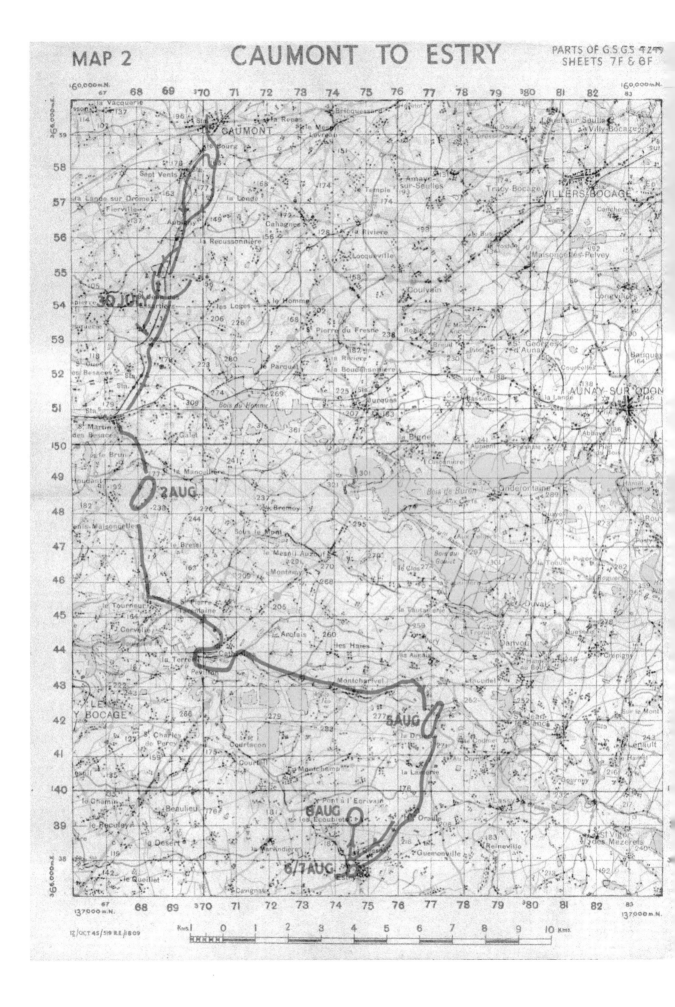

12/OCT 45/519 R.E./1809

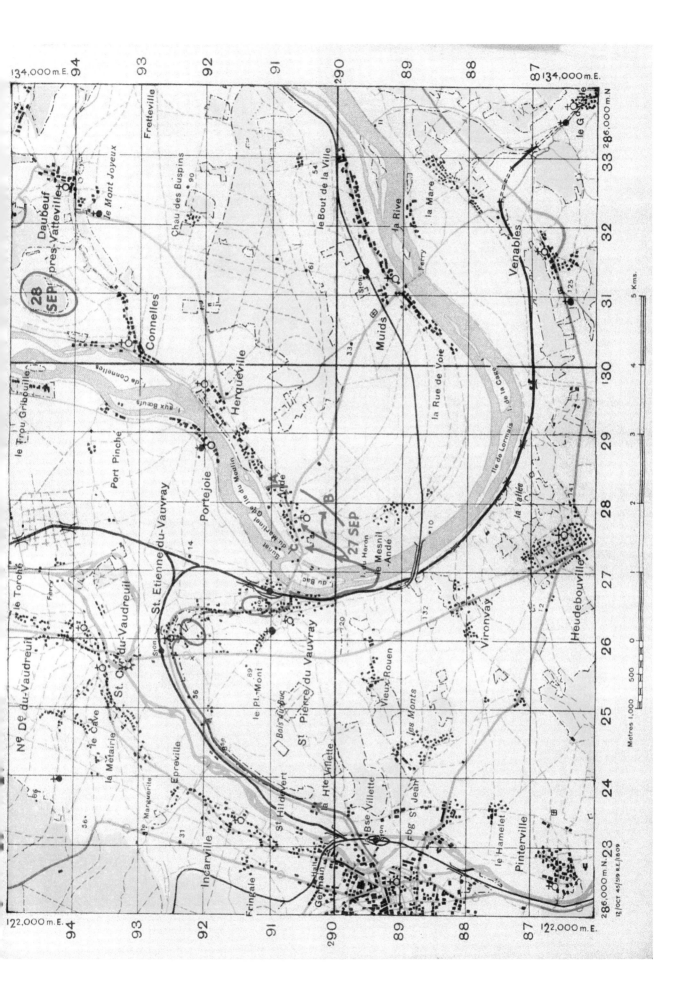

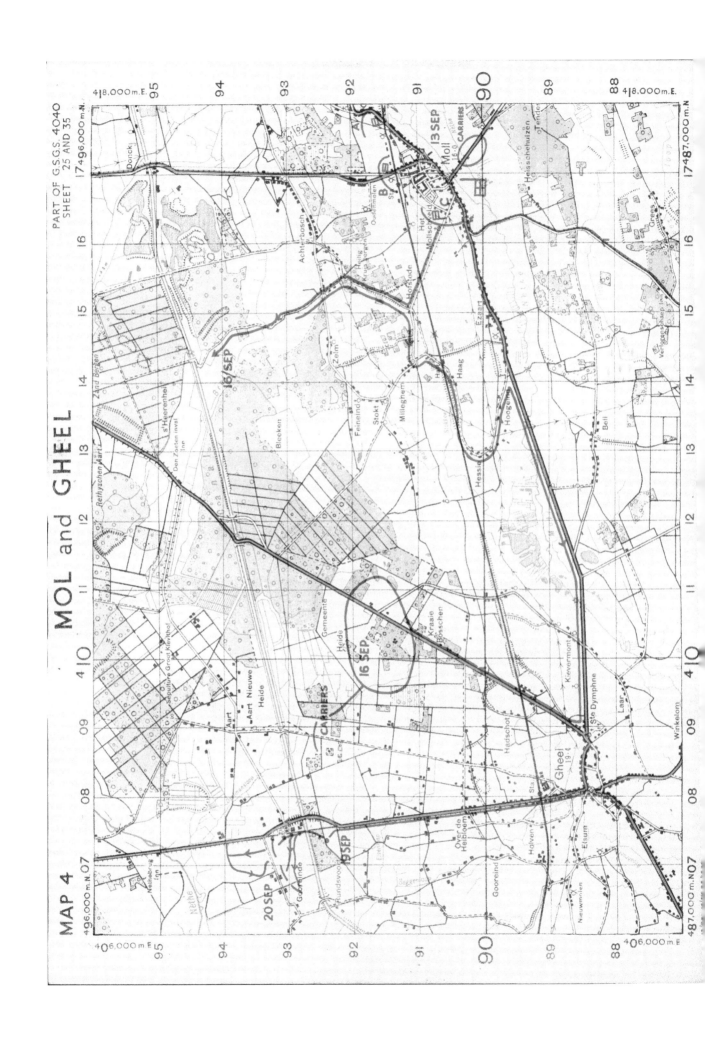

MAP 4

MOL and GHEEL

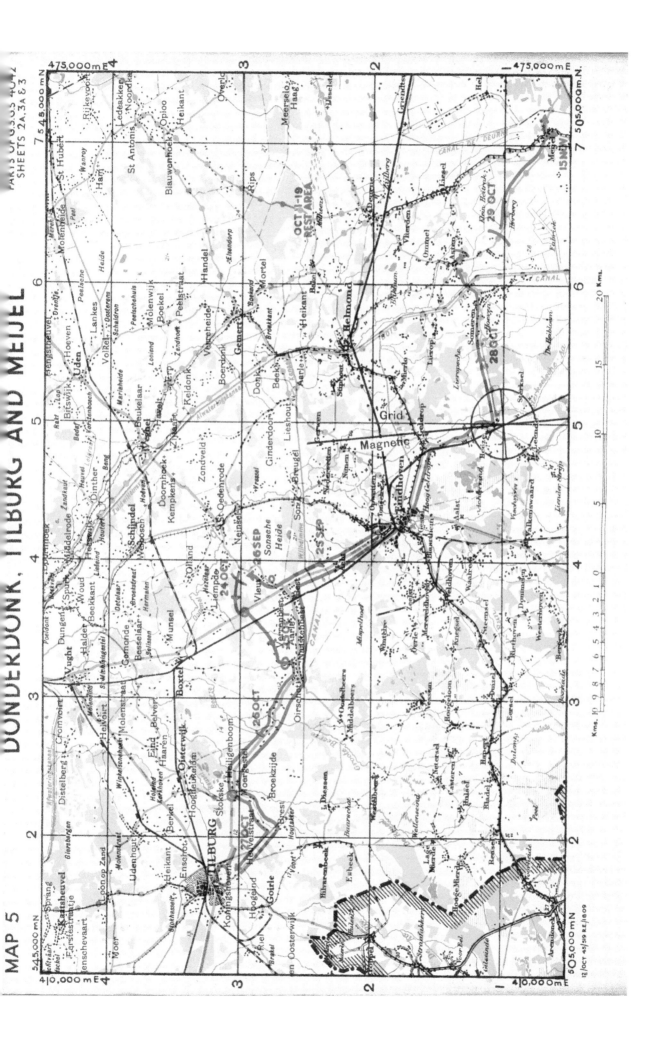

MAP 5

DONDERDONK, TILBURG AND MEIJEL

560,000 m.N.   8   9   500   560,000 m.N.

470,000 m.E.

FORST REICHSWALD

8 FEB · 9 FEB · 11 FEB · 15/18 FEB · 21/24 FEB · 24 MAR · 27 NOV · 7 DEC

470,000 m.E.

500,000 m.N.   8   9   500   500,000 m.N.

515,000 m.E.

12/OCT 45/519 R.E./1809

Kms. 10 9 8 7 6 5 4 3 2 1 0   5   10   15   20 Kms.

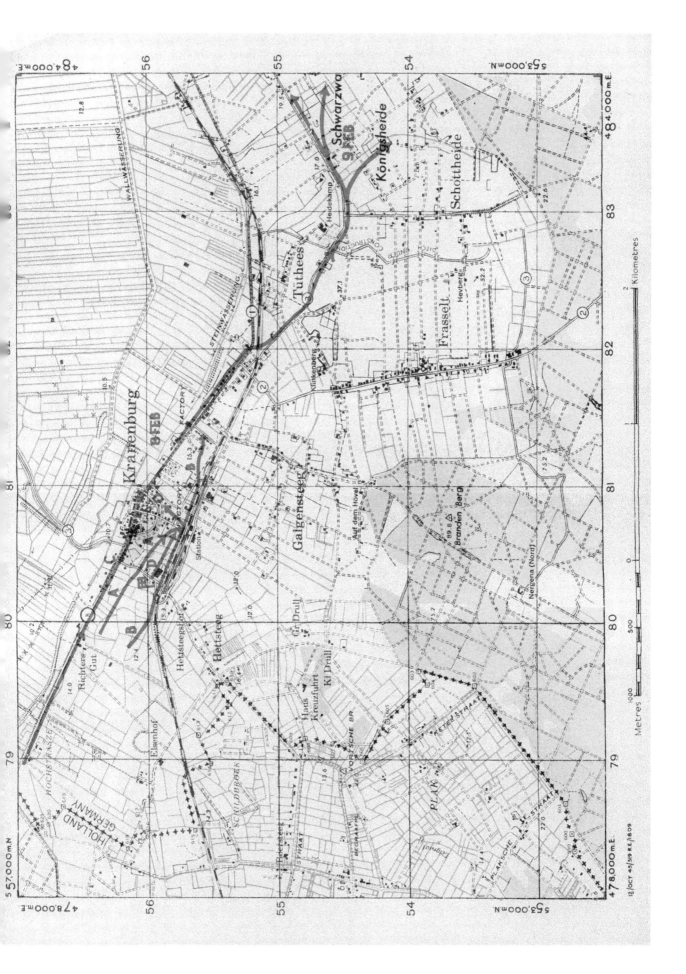

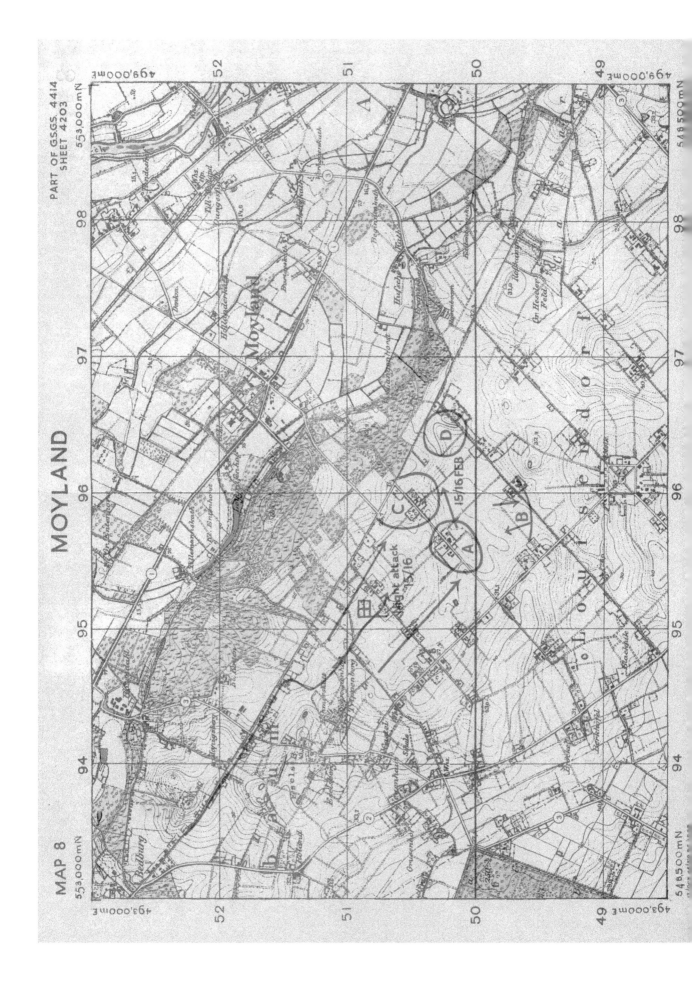

MOYLAND

MAP 8

PART OF G.S.G.S. 4414
SHEET 4203

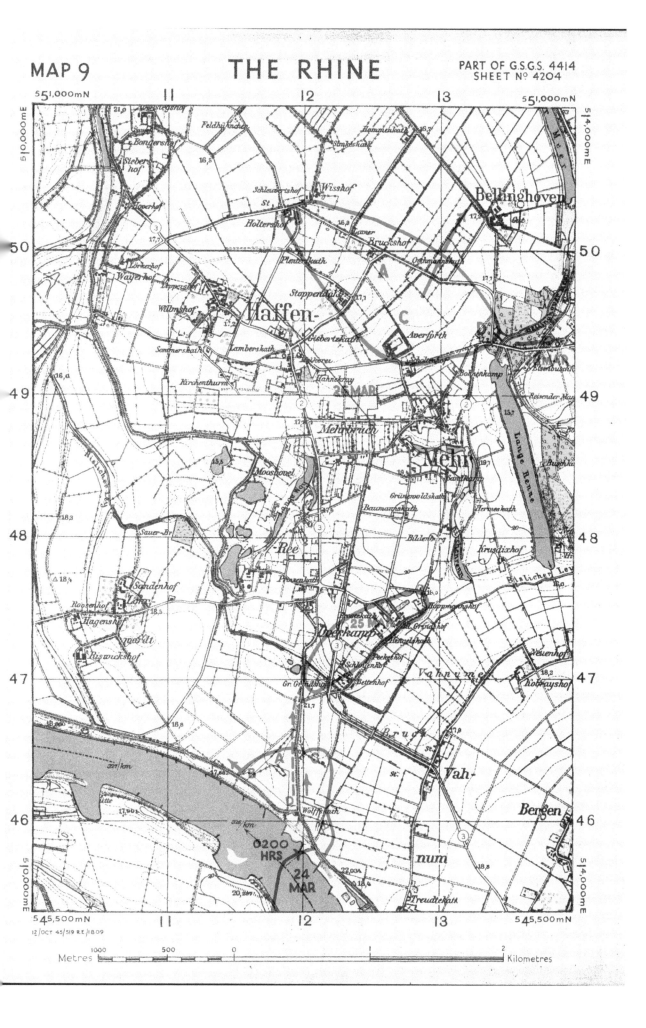

MAP 9   THE RHINE

Metres   1000   500   0   1   2   Kilometres

12/OCT/45/519 R.E./18·09

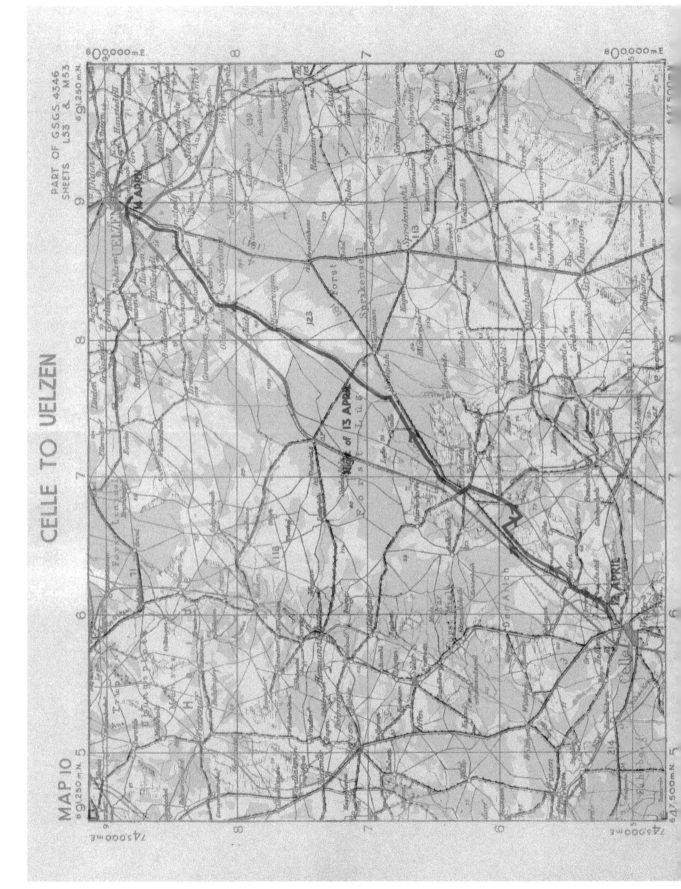

MAP IO

CELLE TO UELZEN

Night of 13 APRIL

14 APRIL

12 APRIL

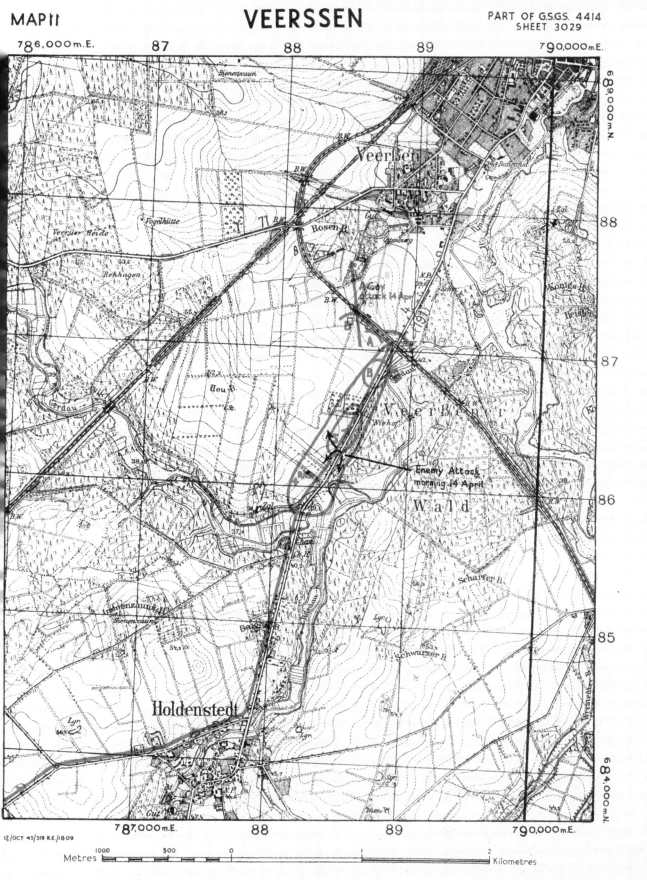

786,000 m.E.   87   88   89   790,000 m.E.

689,000 m.N.

Veerßen

88

87

86

A Coy
Attack 14 Apr

Enemy Attack
morning 14 April

Veerßener

W a l d

85

684,000 m.N.

12/OCT 45/519 R.E./1809

787,000 m.E.   88   89   790,000 m.E.

Holdenstedt

Metres 1000   500   0   1   2   Kilometres

Positions in red show positions taken up subsequent to A Coy's attack on the morning 14 April

Positions in green show night attack on 14/15 April and subsequent dispositions on 15 April

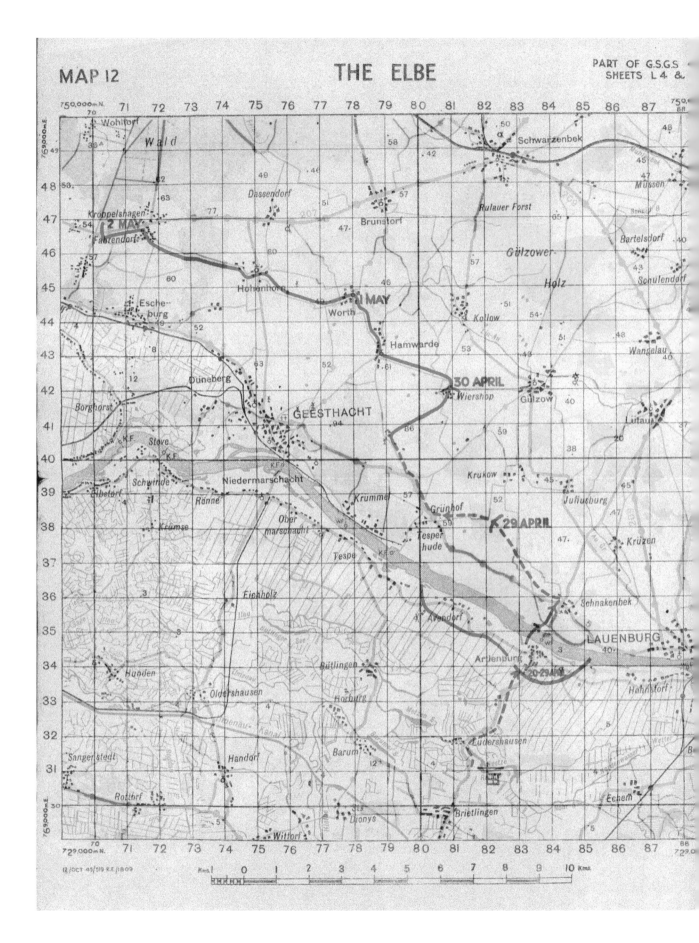

MAP 12

THE ELBE

Lightning Source UK Ltd.
Milton Keynes UK
UKHW050835190822
407497UK00002B/110

9 781783 3